FRU**IT**

defrICtion

UNLEASHING YOUR ENTERPRISE
TO CREATE VALUE FROM CHANGE

CHRIS POTTS

FRUITIon THREE

defrICtion

UNLEASHING YOUR ENTERPRISE
TO CREATE VALUE FROM CHANGE

CHRIS POTTS

Technics Publications
New Jersey

Published by:
Technics Publications, LLC
966 Woodmere Drive
Westfield, NJ 07090
www.technicspub.com

Edited by Carol Lehn
Cover design by Mark Brye

Copyright © 2012 by Technics Publications, LLC
Diagrams copyright by Dominic Barrow Services Limited

ISBN, print ed.	978-1-9355044-6-7
ISBN, Kindle ed.	978-1-9355044-5-0

First Printing 2012
Library of Congress Control Number: 2012951609

To Steve, Mike and Mark
who, back in 2000,
already knew

Contents

Preface

How can we best inspire people to deliver as much value as they can from all the changes we invest in? How much does it depend on the way we plan and execute the changes themselves, on the technologies involved, or on the governance we apply? Maybe it depends on all of these things, or maybe something else.

Thoughts like those began troubling Michael F. Rodgers, Chief Executive Officer (CEO) of a global corporation based in New York City, as he lay in the bathtub late one Wednesday evening, reading the Business Case for a change proposed by one of his Chief Officers. So, as people like Michael often do, he decided to act on these thoughts the very next day.

If you've read RecrEAtion, you've met Michael before. But, that was someone else's story, in which he had a supporting role. This time, he gets to tell his own story, his way. And his way is to tell it as he sees it, and to be provocative when he feels the need.

Michael is, more than anything, a 'people person'. Before he became CEO, he was the company's global Chief Marketing Officer (CMO), so the people he thinks about are as much the company's customers, and potential customers, as its employees and investors. When he's asked what keeps him awake at night, he always answers "the market". Some think to ask him "which one?", to which he unfailingly replies "each and every one of them."

Like many of us, Michael has grown up in business witnessing the relentless changes in our work and our lives caused by the ever-deeper integration of Information Technologies (IT) into both. He has experienced all that comes with being involved in that journey - its exuberances and disillusions, marvels and disasters. And, like many of us, he assumed IT itself to be the cause of the drama, as well as the bête-noire star of the show.

But, thanks to one thought in the bathtub, followed by a dinner conversation in a Manhattan restaurant, his understanding of all that is about to change fundamentally. His dinner guest was none other than Ian Taylor, frontman of FruITion and one-time Chief Information Officer (CIO). Fortunately, that evening, Michael was open to changing his mind, and how he felt, about the subject. Otherwise, it's likely that nothing much else would have changed.

So, without further delay, I'm going to hand you over to Michael. At the end of each stage in his story, I've made some observations about what I think he has told us. As always, I encourage you to make some more observations of your own. I expect you'll notice many different things from me.

DEFRICTION

ONE

Michael

I used to think that the best projects were the ones that delivered their Business Case benefits.

Well, I got that wrong. And I wasn't alone, I can tell you that.

How we all got ourselves into that mess is not what I want to tell you, though. How we pulled ourselves out of it, what that did for the performance of our company and for the motivations of our people - that's what I need you to know.

Think about it. You propose a project. A change to the way we do things. You estimate the costs and the potential benefits based on various hypotheses, other people's experiences of something similar, and guesswork. We give you the go-ahead, then months, or even years later, when the change has been implemented, you deliver the benefits you proposed and for the costs you estimated. Two questions... What's the probability of that happening? And, even if it does happen, is that really the best outcome we could achieve?

Now, don't get me wrong, Business Cases aren't, in and of themselves, a bad idea, otherwise nobody would use them. If you've had an idea for a change you want to make, and are looking for an investment, then you've got to make the case. But, that's the problem. Our portfolio of investments in change will be limited to the changes people want to make, and have managed to convince us to invest in. Knowing what I now know, I'd confidently predict - every time - that a different portfolio would deliver the outcomes we want more efficiently, and quicker. One that starts with our goals and drives us to find the best changes to invest in, rather than starts with changes we want to make and then tries to align them with our goals.

Let me introduce myself. I'm Michael F. Rodgers, Chief Executive Officer (CEO) of a global corporation based in New York City. Before I became CEO, I was the company's global Chief Marketing Officer (CMO). At the beginning of the events I'm going to tell you about, we had 56 subsidiaries worldwide, employing some 125,000 people. Our total annual revenues were around $89 billion, net profits $9.5 billion, and our market capitalization was $64 billion.

As a CEO, I want people to be motivated to deliver the most value they can, as efficiently as they can, from all the investments we make. If we're expecting people to 'make the case for change', then we're driving them to be motivated by change itself. We cause them to behave as agents of change, rather than delivering value from change. Now, there are plenty of agents of change out there in the market - suppliers, consultants, and so on. We need our own people to be agents of value, from stability, or change, or the combination of both. That's what makes a great investment culture.

Investment culture. You wouldn't have found me saying that before the events I'm going to tell you about. Now, it's the foundation of our strategy.

Here's what got me started. Late one Wednesday night, after attending an evening function, I was lying in the bathtub in my Manhattan apartment reading the Business Case for a transformation program. Yes, reading a Business Case in my bathtub in the middle of the night. The program was, on the face of it, primarily about IT. As a result, the Business Case had been prepared by my Chief Technology Officer (CTO), Lucy Hau, and endorsed by my Chief Financial Officer (CFO), Howard Fox. Every Business Case we consider at Board level needs Howard's endorsement. The up-front investment for Lucy's program was $87 million, over three years, and all capitalized expenditure; not a lot of money for a company our size. The program offered a positive five-year NPV[1], which was above our standard threshold for approval. In essence, it was going to bring in more cash than it spent. An easy decision, it seemed.

Had the estimated cost been $86 million, or $88 million, this story might have ended right there. But, I happened to remember reading, somewhere, that $87 million was the amount invested in restoring the Statue of Liberty, back in the 1980s when she was at significant risk of structural failure. You see, alongside my professional life as CEO, I am passionate about New York City, itself, and about history and architecture, in general.

The value of Lucy's transformation program, versus the value of restoring the Statue of Liberty. OK, so $87 million in the 1980s would be worth much more now. But the fact that the two numbers were the same still got me thinking. Was Lucy's transformation the most valuable use of that investment? What else might we do with it?

Then another, related, thought floated into my mind. How would this investment in transforming IT deliver us new cash? Where

---

[1] Net Present Value.

would its promised NPV come from? I tried to assemble that structure in my head. I could see cash flowing out of the door, to pay for the people, products, and services that the program needed. But, I couldn't see how any new cash would flow in, and the Business Case didn't adequately explain it. So, how come it had a positive NPV?

It was getting late and I was a bit drained from the long day I'd had, so perhaps I was being unusually dumb. I decided to sleep on it, have another look in the morning, then talk to Lucy and Howard.

Fresh from an hour in the gym, my first meeting the next morning, at 8 A.M., was with Simon Rathbone. Simon was our Senior Vice President of Enterprise Architecture. Three years before, he'd joined us from a company in London, England. I could tell, as soon as I saw him walk into my office on his first day in the company, that he came with a lot of bottled-up, unfulfilled ambition. Then he made the fortunate mistake of telling me that he did something called 'Enterprise Architecture'. Knowing something about both enterprise and architecture, and as the person who designs the structure of the company, provocatively I told him, "Me, too". It turned out we were talking about different things, but I soon straightened him out. He'd started out working for Lucy, but I changed that within a few days. I'm the chief architect of our enterprise, after all, so anyone working on the structure of the company works for me.

Simon's a walking example of what people can achieve when they're free to express themselves in what they do best. Now, he's my Chief Officer for Enterprise Investment, and I'm driving him to make the role as influential as the CFO. The more we understand and exploit the differences, as well as the overlaps, between finance and investment, the more we need each to have robust representation in the Boardroom. After all, money is not the investment that delivers any value. It took a lot more than $87 million to fix-up Lady Liberty. To my mind, money is usually the easy part, although Howard likes to tell me that's because I'm still a CMO at heart. So far, he's been playing ball with me on our corporate strategy for Enterprise Investment. But, as much as I value Howard, if I ever find out he's been faking it, I'll replace him.

With Simon sitting in front of me, I decided to find out what he would say about my bathtub concerns. As usual, I dove straight in. "I was reading Lucy's Business Case last night. I know you've seen it too. It's NPV-positive. You used to work in IT. How do we get new cash in the bank from an IT transformation?"

"What about if it saves us money?"

"Good question. Nice try. That would mean we could keep cash in the bank we would have otherwise spent, but get no new cash through the door. And, anyway, our corporate strategy is about making more money by growing the company. Increasing profits by saving money was my predecessor's strategy. First-and-foremost we need revenue growth, both now and into the future. So, if you're right, and Lucy is going to deliver us some cash savings, we can either wait until she does, and then invest them in changes that deliver us revenue, or take the $87 million she wants and simply invest it in growing revenues now. Jam tomorrow, or jam today. Hey, I'm answering my own question. I wanted to hear what you would say."

"Hold on, Michael. I'm playing catch-up. Why are you asking me this?" Good, I thought, I don't like it when I'm the one playing catch-up.

"OK," I replied, "Lucy's Business Case is promising to deliver a positive NPV from an up-front capital investment of $87 million. As Howard likes to remind me, I'm not a Finance guy. I was trying to figure out how we would deliver Lucy's NPV from an IT transformation, before talking to Howard and to Lucy herself, and feeling stupid if there's an obvious answer. Now I'm starting to wonder if what I've noticed about

Lucy's proposal might be true of other changes we invest in. Why do all our Business Cases promise a positive NPV? I don't see a flood of new cash coming from all the projects we finish. Anyway, there are all kinds of reasons we invest in change, most of which generate no cash whatsoever."

I stopped talking, because Simon, suddenly, appeared to be someplace else. Looking at me, but not. I gave him a couple of seconds then asked, "What just happened? Where did you just go?"

"Serendipity."

"Tell me. Before it goes."

"You just talked about NPV. Tomorrow I'm having lunch with Ian Taylor, my old boss from London. He's over here for a conference."

"What's the connection?"

"When I worked with Ian, he was the company's Chief Information Officer, the CIO. Then, our Chief Executive, Juliette, suddenly took him out of IT and got him looking at the company's strategy for Investing in Change. I heard he had a bit of a problem with Finance. At the heart of the problem was NPV. That's about all I know. I wasn't directly involved."

"Right. What's his schedule? Can I talk to him?"

"Apart from seeing him for lunch, I don't know. I'll call him and say you'd like to see him."

"Thanks. If he's willing, get Trudy to sort out something. Dinner would be best." Trudy is my Personal Assistant.

Simon left to sort that out, and I decided to hold-off my conversations with Howard and Lucy until I had spoken with this guy, Ian Taylor. I sincerely hoped it would be a dinner well spent. Time is my most valuable asset.

Observations

- Investments are based on hypotheses, previous experiences, and guesswork

- Start with your goals and find the best changes to invest in, rather than start with changes people want to make and align them with your goals

- We need our people to be agents of delivering value from change, not agents of change itself

- Your enterprise's investment culture is the foundation of your strategy for creating value from change

- Make sure everyone understands the differences between finance and investment

- There are many reasons for investing in change that generate no financial return.

TWO

Ian

"I think your problem," he said, "is that your problem isn't what you think it is."

Up to that moment, I was enjoying our conversation, and Ian had seemed like a straight-talking kind of guy. Now, suddenly, he'd turned into a riddler.

I'd taken it from Simon that his old friend was worth investing my time in, to talk about my Business Case question. Trudy had booked us a table for the evening at my favorite small restaurant in New York's East Village. Six months afterwards, I was sad to see it shut down. Yet it was always popular, and had great on-line reviews. The owners must have made some big misjudgements in their numbers, their politics, or both.

As I prefer to do, I made sure we waited until dessert before talking business. Then, I decided to start with Ian's history and his sudden change in role. I'll return to his riddle in a moment.

"Simon told me you used to be a CIO."

"Yes, I did."

"I don't have a CIO. Should I? I've got a CTO named Lucy, who looks after our IT. Is she the same as a CIO?"

"Depends on who you ask. I wouldn't worry about it, if I were you. Are you happy with her leadership?"

"Yes." At least, enough not to talk to a stranger about it.

"Then leave it like that. Anyway, that's not why I think I'm here."

"OK. Keep going."

Ian asked, "Can we talk about Simon for a moment?"

"What about him?"

"I know he's leading your strategy for Enterprise Architecture. He told me that, when I last saw him in London, shortly before his mother died..."

I interrupted, "I didn't know his mother died. When did that happen?"

"About two years ago. Simon's sometimes very private about family matters. I wanted to say that what you've done for him is amazing.

He's a different person from the Simon I used to know."

"I doubt it. What he's achieved, he's done himself. I just helped him remove some of his roadblocks. His fiancée is good for him too - and vice versa." Simon was engaged to a Canadian, Françoise, whom he met working for me. They're married now, with a baby on the way.

Ian continued. "Simon has a knack for triggering reactions in others..."

"Tell me about it. But I think he only started to realize that quite recently, and is figuring out how to use it to influence people's behaviors in the ways that he wants."

"You're right. He often used to influence people to do the opposite of what he wanted. Anyway, I lead strategies for Investing in Change. Simon's leading your strategy for Enterprise Architecture. He started me thinking about what would happen if we put those two strategies together."

I told Ian that was an interesting idea, and that if we had time, we would come back to it later. As he started to eat his dessert, I told him about my Business Case moment, and the follow-up conversation with Simon. So far, each time I listened to myself tell someone, the more convinced I became that there must be something wrong. To make matters worse, when I had finished telling this guy what I was thinking, he seemed to take no notice. He just carried on eating his dessert.

"Well. What do you think?" I asked him, frustrated with his lack of reaction. Gently, he put down his spoon and fork, touched his mouth with his napkin, and spoke his riddle about my problem not being what I thought it was.

"What's that supposed to mean?" I asked him.

"What do you think the problem is?" he countered.

"Do you mean with the Business Case, or our conversation?"

"Exactly. If you want to get the most from your investments in change, your Business Case is triggering the wrong conversation. Before it gets written, in whatever context it gets agreed to or rejected, and throughout the entire investment process."

"Hold on there, friend. Are you saying there's something as simple as a document making things go wrong across our entire structure?"

"It could well be. But that's not what I'm saying. I expect the core of your problem isn't structural. It's cultural."

"Go on."

"What can you tell me about the investment culture of your company?"

I looked Ian in the eye. Said nothing. I could hear myself breathing.

"I don't get what you're asking me." I admitted, with difficulty.

"OK. What are you doing tomorrow? Do you have an hour? I'd like to show you something that will answer the question I just asked you. Then we can talk again about Business Cases, CIOs, and CTOs, if you still want to."

He had me hooked enough to want to know more.

"Breakfast. My office. Eight A.M. Is that OK?"

"Yes."

I called over the waitress, ordered two coffees, and the check.

I asked Ian, "You're an American, right?"

"Yes, but I've lived in England for years."

"I can tell by the accent. You kinda sound English here, but I expect you still sound American in England. So, where are you from, originally?"

"California, Illinois, and Ohio, mainly. We moved around when I was a kid. My father was in the Air Force."

"I'm from right here."

"New York?"

"East Village. This may sound like a strange question, but do you like rock music?"

"Yes, I do. Why?"

I asked him if he knew the Led Zeppelin album, Physical Graffiti.

"I certainly do."

"The cover photo. We lived there for a while."

"In one of those houses?"

"Nearly. On the same street."

"Wow." After a short pause, Ian continued, "There's a track on that album called In the Light."

"Yes, there is. What of it?"

"Well, let's see if I can help shine some more on the subject tomorrow."

"Very good. Very good."

As we finished our coffees and I paid the waitress, I asked Ian why he wanted to help me.

"For Simon. And what you've done for him. And because I want to see what's around the next bend in the road. What happens when you join Enterprise Architecture and Investing in Change together, into one strategy, with one Chief Officer. If that's what you choose to do."

"OK. Let's talk tomorrow morning about putting those two strategies together."

The next morning I left the gym a few minutes early to make sure I was prepared for the meeting with Ian. When I got to my office, he and our breakfast were waiting outside. Trudy bought them both in.

After we had wished each other good morning, he reached for his iPad and placed it between us on my meeting table. On the screen was something that looked like a matrix. Without waiting for me to ask, he said, "This is going to be a one-page diagnosis of your company's investment culture. It should take about fifteen minutes to complete, then we can talk about what it means."

Here is what was showing on his screen:

Investment Culture Diagnosis

Dimension	Prevailing Culture			
Value Creation	Considered Always	Considered Last	Avoided	Considered First
Innovation Focus	None	Market	Technical	Internal
Investment Portfolio	Inventory	Bottom-Up	Non-Existent	Top-Down
Targeting	Outcomes	Activities	Outputs	None
Exploiting Assets & Services	Central	Missing	Peripheral	Intended
Investment Strategy	Random	Strategic Goals	Operational Goals	Something Else
Sponsorship	Accountable	Nominal	Absent	Responsible
Project Management	Delivering Change	Time/Cost/Quality	ROI Hypothesis	Delivering Value
Impact on Operating Costs	Important	Ignored	Interesting	Critical
Behavior Towards Projects	Controlling	Influencing	Undermining	Not Interested

"Let me explain what you're looking at. Down the left hand side are ten dimensions of your investment culture. I'm sure there are more, but these always seem to be enough. They are in no particular order. For each of them, there are four possible ways of describing your prevailing culture. Within each row, they are also not in any order."

"Why's that?"

"So there's no obvious pattern to influence your answers."

"What if our prevailing culture fits with more than one answer?"

"You can have up to two answers per row. More than that, and we'll lose sight of what it's telling us. Now, I'm going to talk you through each row, and you're going to choose the one or two answers that best describe your culture."

"How can you be sure my answers will be right?"

"More often than not they will be. You know your enterprise. But, if you want to make this really interesting, get each of your executives to do the diagnosis individually, and compare your answers. I'll send you an uncompleted version when we've finished."

"I guess I have to answer with what I know to be true, rather than what I'd like it to be."

"Indeed. That's essential."

"I'm ready."

"OK. Let's start."

Ian described each row, and I chose one or two answers each time. I've reproduced his descriptions at the end of my story, to save repeating them here. He picked out my answers on his iPad. When we had finished, the Diagnosis looked like this:

Investment Culture Diagnosis

Dimension	Prevailing Culture			
Value Creation	Considered Always	Considered Last	Avoided	Considered First
Innovation Focus	None	Market	Technical	Internal
Investment Portfolio	Inventory	Bottom-Up	Non-Existent	Top-Down
Targeting	Outcomes	Activities	Outputs	None
Exploiting Assets & Services	Central	Missing	Peripheral	Intended
Investment Strategy	Random	Strategic Goals	Operational Goals	Something Else
Sponsorship	Accountable	Nominal	Absent	Responsible
Project Management	Delivering Change	Time/Cost/Quality	ROI Hypothesis	Delivering Value
Impact on Operating Costs	Important	Ignored	Interesting	Critical
Behavior Towards Projects	Controlling	Influencing	Undermining	Not Interested

He put the iPad in front of me, and asked, "Well, what do you see?" Despite the page having no apparent pattern, I could still notice one in my answers.

"I see that we have a culture focused on the execution of change, one project at time. I say that because we have targets based on activities and outputs, our project management is about the delivery of change and measured by time/cost/quality, and our portfolio is really no more than an inventory."

"Interesting," Ian commented, "anything else?"

"Yes. We're interested in the creation of value at the beginning of the investment and at the end, with Business Cases and Benefits Realization, but we lose sight of it in between. And some other things, but they're the main ones."

"Your answer to Investment Strategy is 'Something Else'. What is that?"

"Net Present Value."

Ian smiled. "Ah yes, an old buddy of mine. If buddy is the right word."

"Simon said something about that."

"NPV is great if you're investing cash, to get cash in return. The changes that enterprises invest in aren't like that. We invest a lot of time, as well as cash, and want - most often - something other than cash in return. Out of interest, how much actual cash did your change projects consume and deliver last year, compared to their proposed NPVs?"

"I don't know those numbers, but I get what you're saying," I said, feeling on the defensive. "I'll check with our CFO."

Ian dropped that subject and returned to the Investment Culture Diagnosis. "If you could choose one thing to change, what would it be?"

"Why only one thing? Forget I asked. I know how difficult it can be to change a culture. I'd like us to focus on value creation throughout the entire process of investing in change. It's usually a long and eventful journey between approving the Business Case and realizing the benefits. All sorts of things go wrong if we take our eye off the ball."

"Too true. And how would you want to achieve that? After all, it's not something you can just go and do."

I thought about what he said, looked again at his iPad, and noticed something about the page we had just completed. Despite Ian saying there was no apparent pattern, behind it all there was clearly some kind of causes-and-effects structure. If our focus on value creation is an effect, and the one that I wanted to change, what could I use as my cause?

"I can see you looking at the causes-and-effects." he said. "Would you like me to suggest something?"

"Wait."

He waited.

"Project Management," I said. "We're managing projects as implementations, not investments."

"That's very common, in my experience."

"I'm not sure whether that's good news, or bad. At least we're not alone in messing this up. But surely it means that the people we need will be difficult to find?"

"I never said you were messing it up. But now we're getting to the truth about what's stopping you from getting the most from your investments in change. I'll bet you don't prioritize your projects based on the availability - or scarcity - of investment managers."

"No. We prioritize them on..."

I stopped. I didn't want to say the answer.

Ian said it instead. "I know. Net Present Value."

"That's right."

"But now it doesn't really matter whether the NPV in the Business Case is right or not. Let me develop this further. How much does the probability of success feature in your selection and management of investments?"

"Probability? We don't ask that in our Business Cases, either."

"Then you may well be caught in what we call the 'Project Probability Paradox'. That refers to a culture where the higher a project's probability of getting investment, the lower its probability of success. Typically, people have to 'justify' their projects by claiming as much value as they can. Of course, the more value you claim you will deliver, the less probable it is you'll deliver it. In an Investment Culture Diagnosis like yours, where Value Creation is Considered First and Considered Last, the actual probability of achieving the project's value proposition - or any value at all - only comes to light at the end. In cultures where the Diagnosis is Considered First and nothing else, then the actual probability may never come to light."

"I can see that," I commented.

"Where I come from, probability drives our project management and governance from the very beginning to the end, and at all times in between. We demand absolute transparency from people on whether the probabilities of success are going up or down. Where success is getting the value we want from the investment, in exchange for its costs to P&L[2]."

"The costs to P&L? Not the up-front capital investment?"

"I don't care, generally, whether it's capital or not. Remember, I'm an investment guy not a finance guy. I'm interested in getting the most value from all the investments we make, whatever we're investing. And, anyway, we can only deliver the value of a change when it's been implemented, and impacting our operating costs."

I looked again at the diagnosis of our Investment Culture. I'd chosen 'Interesting' for the impact of changes on our operating costs. From what Ian was telling me, it seemed that we might need to make that 'Critical'.

Our conversations over dinner and breakfast had already given me much to consider. We had about 20 minutes left of the hour I'd allowed, so I took the conversation back to the idea he'd mentioned the previous evening, of a combined strategy for Enterprise Architecture and Investing in Change.

---

[2] Profit and Loss

"Why do you think it's a good thing to do?" I asked him.

He explained that a strategy for Investing in Change focuses on the value produced by the portfolio. A good strategy for Enterprise Architecture focuses on the structure produced by the portfolio. It's the same portfolio in both cases. A merged strategy would focus on both the value and structure that investments produce.

"What would you call the merged strategy?"

"Enterprise Investment. And you'll need a Chief Officer as influential as the CFO to lead it."

"I can see that. I may as well ask. Could it be you?"

"No, I'm heading home to Europe. But it could be Simon."

I asked Ian if there was anything else I should know.

He said that Business Cases can be a valuable stepping-stone towards great management of investments in change, but they are not the end of the journey. "Take a careful look at the questions you ask, and - believe me, this is really important - the sequence in which you're asking them. I expect you're asking most of the right questions, but not necessarily in the right order. Also, now you've gotten this far, you're best changing the name from Business Case to Investment Proposal. You're asking people to start in the wrong place, to create an investment out of a change, rather than the other way around."

"I get the name change, but what questions should we be asking and in which order?"

"OK, here's a quick summary of the questions, in the right order. What outcome are you proposing? How much will it cost us? How, in reality, will we achieve it? What's the probability of success? If you don't like the answer to the first question, don't bother with the second one, and so on."

"Right."

He also said to check that we had all the capabilities we needed to successfully get from the beginning to the end of our investment process. The beginning, he said, is where someone has an idea, "Like you did, in the bathtub," and the end is where the idea has either been exploited as much as possible, or we've exited the process. Exploit or exit. The two ways out of an investment.

Finally, Ian came back to the subject of Lucy and IT that I'd first raised over dinner the night before. "There was a time when IT was centered on what employees do and how that affects the value a company creates. These days, now that the IT market has become consumerized, the main focus has to be external. What employees do with IT is still important, but what customers, investors, and other people out there are doing with IT, that needs to be driving your decision and actions. So, where Lucy is proposing investments involving IT, make sure she's applying that change of focus. In an increasing number of cases, you should find that your enterprise makes changes that exploit IT, but have little or no new IT investment."

"Why's that?" I asked him.

"Because you don't pay for the IT that consumers are using, either to enhance your company's value or destroy it."

"True. Nor the IT our employees own and use for their work. That sounds like a conversation I need to have with Howard, as much as Lucy. He's still expecting her to account for the value we create from the IT budget. But, you're right. There're lots of people using IT in ways that impact the value of our company but don't appear in that budget."

"It sounds like your CFO might be at least a generation behind the game."

"Oh." I commented, wondering whether my CTO was, too. "How would I know?"

"The best way to tell which generation you are is to notice which strategic conversation you predominantly have in the Boardroom with your CIO or CTO."

"How many generations are there?"

"There are four generations of CIO strategy. They're being driven by major inflections in the IT market. Right now, the market as a whole is in generation three. Around the world, there are still many Boardrooms, and their CIOs, stuck in generation two - or even one."

Ian tapped a few times on his iPad and showed me this:

The Four Generations of CIO Strategy

Generation Four Enterprise Investment	Strategic conversation: **Delivering value & structure through investing in change**
↑	
Generation Three IT Exploitation	Strategic conversation: **People creating value from investments involving IT**
↑	
Generation Two IT Efficiency	Strategic conversation: **IT budgets & services, sourcing & delivery**
↑	
Generation One Technology	Strategic conversation: **IT Architecture & Technology Roadmap**

I observed, "Now I can see why you're saying our CFO might be a generation behind the market. I think, as a Board, we all might be."

"Right. It's worth bearing in mind that the value you get from your IT budget is becoming a redundant conversation."

"Because of the consumerization of the IT market."

"More than anything, yes."

At this point, Trudy came into my office, to remind me of my next meeting. I had one last question for Ian. "So, Generation Four is 'Enterprise Investment'. You've talked about having a Chief Officer for that. But, these are the four generations of CIO strategy. Help me. Do we need a CIO as well?"

"A Chief Officer for Enterprise Investment is the role formerly known as CIO, when it reaches its fourth-generation destiny. Your background is in Brand, right?"

I nodded.

"When you hear or read 'CIO' what do you immediately think of?"

"IT."

"Exactly. You mentioned roadblocks yesterday evening. For CIOs who want to move onwards and upwards, that's a roadblock."

I thanked Ian for his help. It had been a fascinating hour. He emailed me, there and then, the completed Investment Culture Diagnosis, an uncompleted version, and his Four Generations picture.

As he stood up to leave, he pitched one of his people to me. "I have an experienced investment portfolio manager who is looking for their next job in the States. Would you like me to put you in touch?"

"Tell him to email me with your name as the Subject. I'll make sure Trudy is expecting it."

"Her. Rebecca Chekhova."

"Is she from IT, like you and Simon?"

Ian frowned at me, looking offended, and then said, "No, Wall Street. She has spent the last four years in London and wants to come home."

"OK. Show her the diagnosis. I'll want to know what she would do to change our culture."

Observations

- The way you expect people to propose an investment can trigger the right, or wrong, conversations and behaviors

- Many investment cultures are focused on the execution of change, one project at a time

- A portfolio is more than an inventory of projects

- In a mature investment culture, probabilities drive the selection, end-to-end management, and governance of projects

- The Project Probability Paradox: the higher the probability of getting investment, the lower the probability of success

- Exploit or exit - the two ways out of an investment.

THREE

Simon

Simon's Achilles heel was, when I met him and probably before, a lack of self-confidence. Except when he thought he was right and someone else wrong; then he was too confident by far. To my mind, there are two kinds of people - those who believe in themselves, and those who don't. Which of these you are, all-in-all, determines how well you make it in life.

What I've most worked with Simon to adjust is recognizing the difference between what is technically right and politically wise, and doing so before he acts, rather than afterwards. In the early days, when he was new to the company, I had to risk some of my own political capital to support him in situations he should never have provoked. To this day, he doesn't know, and I have no plans to tell him.

After my dinner and breakfast with Ian Taylor, I had to park those thoughts and conversations for a few days. Among other things, I had a main Board meeting, a briefing call with the investment analysts on Wall Street, and a serious issue with our subsidiary in France. Over there, we were merging two businesses - one we had grown and the other acquired. We were having major problems with the people from each of them still acting as separate cultures, over a year after the transaction was completed. So I flew to Paris and took Simon with me. It was an architectural problem, after all, if we had one enterprise behaving as two and impacting performance, as a result. Ideally, we would have also taken Sam Hilton with us, my SVP of Human Resources, but he was away in the Far East.

In person, we told our French management what we expected them to do, and reiterated our support for them in achieving it. Between Simon and me, in private, we decided to give them two months. If things weren't looking much better by then, we would put in a new CEO and HR Director, possibly doing an exchange with another of our businesses. The guys in Paris were good at managing stable operations, but evidently not culture change, mergers, or both. To my mind they hadn't decided which culture defined the new enterprise, whether it was one of the original two or a third one, and so couldn't robustly inspire their people to live it.

On the Air France flight back to New York (I always like to travel on the airline of the country I'm visiting), I found the time to tell Simon what I'd learned from his old friend.

"He misses you, you know."

"Me, too. We go back a long way. But, I've never understood why he cut me out of the last strategy he did when we were still working together. I was his strategy manager."

"I didn't know that. Would you like me to speculate?"

"No. That's OK. Thanks, anyway. What did you get from your dinner conversation?"

"Dinner and breakfast. We found another hour the next day. Before I say any more, thank you for the introduction. I'm still digesting what came of it. He took me through a rapid diagnosis of our investment culture. Based on what that showed, no wonder we've got problems creating value from change."

"Did you sort out the NPV question?"

"Yes. No. Ian persuaded me that, while I'm technically right, it's not the main problem I should be thinking about."

"What is?"

"The fact that we're managing projects as implementations rather than investments."

"But, aren't they both?"

"Yes. But it's the investment project that delivers value. The implementation project delivers change. If our projects don't have investment managers, the Business Case can say whatever it likes, about NPV or anything else. Nobody's truly accountable for achieving it."

"But we've got project sponsors."

"Tell me: when was the last time we gave one of them a reward for a successful investment, or a penalty for the opposite? Anyway, a sponsor isn't the same as a dedicated investment manager."

"But, we're doing what best practice tells us to. Most people do it this way."

"I don't care. And, you've started saying 'but' to everything I say. It's irritating me. Anyway, that's a contradiction. If most people are doing something, it can't be best practice."

That seemed to silence him for a moment. He knows I hate apologies, whether for irritating me or anything else. I reckoned he could have probably found an argument, technically, with my last statement. It was good see him think about it instead.

Simon asked me what else Ian had said. I told him about the idea of combining Enterprise Architecture with Investing in Change, to create a single corporate strategy for Enterprise Investment.

"Wow. Who would I report to?"

"Me. I asked Ian if he was fishing to be my Chief Officer for Enterprise Investment, and he recommended you instead."

At this, Simon unleashed a four-letter expletive that I won't repeat here. I continued, "He is also getting one of his people who's looking for a move back to New York to contact me. If she's good, she could be your new SVP of Investing in Change. That would just leave us needing your replacement as SVP of Enterprise Architecture. I think we know who that could be".

"Ivan."

"Ivan. He's done a fantastic job of turning into reality your idea to make us a 'cloud organization'."

"Yes, he has."

"So, if I made you a Chief Officer right now, what would you say?"

"Sometimes, I still find it hard to know whether you're joking or not."

"I'm not joking, but I think there a few things you need to work on first. For a start, you would have to act as an equal to Howard." Another expletive, to which I replied, "Exactly."

I asked Simon what he knew about Rebecca Chekovha, who had fired over an introductory email while he and I were in France. He didn't know her.

"Let's get her on Skype," I suggested, "find out what she's like, what she knows, and whether Ian's taste in people these days is anything like ours. If she's good, we'll get her over in person."

Trudy arranged the date and time. When it arrived, Simon and I sat in the Boardroom to use the big screen in there.

Hard eyes. That's the first thing I noticed. An observation, not a criticism. Depending on what the lady used them for, either an asset or a liability.

"Thank you for your time, Rebecca," I said. "What did you make of the diagnosis?"

"Please call me Becky. Your Diagnosis looks like most people's before they sort themselves out. You're calling an inventory of projects a portfolio and judging them each on their own merits. Diversification within the portfolio is happening by accident rather than design. It's likely to be inefficient in achieving your goals, if it achieves them at all. Very pre-1952."

Straight-talking, as well as hard-eyed.

"What does that mean?" asked Simon.

I wrote on my notepad, "Provocative!" and made sure Simon saw it.

Becky continued, "I'll explain the reference to 1952 in a moment, Simon. Before that I have a question of you both. Do people in your company expect every project to be successful?"

An echo of the probability conversation with Ian. Simon responded again. "Yes, they do, when there's an approved Business Case."

I intervened, deliberately switching the language away from Business Cases. "Ian and I talked about that when he was here. Probability is missing from our Investment Proposals."

"From your investment culture, more like. And which is it – Business Cases or Investment Proposals?"

"At the moment, Business Cases. And I get the point about culture. Now, as Simon already asked you, what's the reference to 1952?"

"Modern Portfolio Theory. Harry Markowitz. Set goals for investment; diversify the portfolio until no more diversity makes it more efficient."

I said, "I get the reference now."

Becky continued, "Good. Then, because we - and the people we invest in - are not always as rational as we'd theoretically like everyone to be, we overlay behavioral economics. Investment portfolio meets investment culture. Do you want me to carry on?"

"Wait a moment," I said, "we have a corporate strategy that's driven by productivity, rather than efficiency. You referred to a portfolio being efficient. Is that a conflict?"

"No. The goals drive the portfolio. That's what it has to produce. If it doesn't, it's unproductive. I was referring to the portfolio being risk-efficient. An efficient portfolio is one that achieves your goals with minimum overall risk."

"OK," I said, "but how does diversification work for investments in change?"

"We diversify the portfolio using the different types of value that people invest in change to achieve."

"Such as?"

"Well, it's up to each enterprise to decide what they are, but there's a generic list we usually start with."

"Keep going."

"OK, here's a list for a commercial enterprise. Government agencies are different. Revenue protection and growth. Cost control and reduction. Productivity. Brand reputation. Customer delight. Employee satisfaction. Legal and regulatory compliance. Enterprise Architecture. Survival. For an actual company, we'll customize these, if they want, and can always add a few more. As a rule of thumb, we plan for between ten and twelve. Any more, and you're diversifying too much. Any less, too little. I've seen people try to work with just four. Nightmare."

Interesting, I thought. I decided to delve some more. "Do those value types also form the basis of our investment goals?"

"Yes. To express them as goals, you need to choose measures of success, a timescale, and targets. The measures will, themselves, be diverse, to match the value types. For example, you'll measure Revenue and Cost as dollars, Productivity as a ratio, Compliance as 'yes/no', and Enterprise Architecture using design characteristics. You can't, realistically, use one measure for all your investments in change."

"OK. So let's check that I've understood. We use a diverse range of value types to set our goals for investing in change. That gives us the foundation for our portfolio. Then we distribute our investments across those goals to maximize risk-efficiency."

"Yes. And, it's worth remembering that your portfolio will also be inefficient if you're investing in goals you could have achieved anyway. For example, by better exploiting existing investments."

"OK. I understand. I'm comfortable with efficient in that context. Let's carry on."

Simon took over the conversation again. "If our company has an investment culture like many others, can you tell us what to do about it?"

"Sure. One of two approaches. Either work on it as part of other culture changes you're making, or deal with it directly. Both can succeed. Being culture change, both are risky. The first one is often easier, but less overt. People won't be so tuned-in to what's changing, and why. I can achieve success either way, and I'd much rather do it than talk about it."

Knowing that Becky could see us, I looked at Simon and nodded. He said, "We'd like to see you in New York. Can you make it here?"

"Easy. I travel all over. Home is where the work is."

I was starting to like Becky Chekhova. A lot.

She continued, "When were you thinking?"

"Talk to Trudy, my PA. See if you can get here in the next couple of weeks."

"Sure."

"We'll cover your travel expenses. Stay over. We'll have dinner. Maybe the three of us, maybe four."

"Who's the fourth one?"

"Ivan. He's an Enterprise Architect."

Although the on-screen image of Becky wasn't quite crystal clear, I was sure her mouth hardened at that moment, to match her eyes. That left me wondering: what was it she didn't want to say?

After we had finished the video call with Becky, Simon and I stayed briefly in the Boardroom, and I asked him to tell me what he'd observed.

"Impressive. Direct. Some people could find her intimidating. All good. But I reckon she doesn't like Enterprise Architects. That could give us a problem."

"I'm with you on all of that. Let's dig into her feelings about Enterprise Architects when we meet her. Make sure Ivan is there to hear what she says and to challenge her, if need be. I'll have a chat with him and get him ready." Simon knows I run an open style of management. Although he's Ivan's SVP, I'll talk to whomever I like, and whenever I want to. "Now," I continued, "back to my office. I'm about to ask Lucy to explain her Business Case, and there's something I'm still not sure of, which seems relevant to all of this."

Simon asked what that was.

"The difference between a CIO and CTO, and which - if either - we really need. I asked Ian, and he told me about the four generations of CIO strategy. But he never answered the CTO question. So I'm going to ask you."

When we arrived back in my office, Simon started the conversation by saying, "The difference between a CIO and a CTO depends on who you ask."

"That's what Ian said. I'm asking you, so go on. Think out loud, if you need to."

"Alright. Both have traditionally been positioned as IT leaders. The CIO is considered more senior than the CTO. Any differences are not treated as fundamental. Surveys of CIOs include CTOs. As far as I know there are no conferences for CIOs where CTOs are barred from attending, nor would find they're out of touch with the content. And, although the I in CIO means Information, that's not usually what the role is all about. Actually, while the T in CTO means Technology, it's only IT. Other technologies are usually handled by someone else."

"So, neither role is really what it says it is. No wonder the rest of us get confused. Is Lucy really our CIO or our CTO?"

"Yes."

"Cute answer. Not helpful."

"Sure. But my point is that I don't think it matters. The CIO/CTO debate is being overtaken by events. IT has become so pervasive to everything, that having its own, separate, management structure is looking increasingly counter-productive. Our management of IT needs to be as pervasive as IT itself. Did Ian tell you what they did with his IT management team when they took him out of the CIO role?"

"No. Tell me."

"The CEO and the Strategy Director took each IT-related capability and integrated it into the most relevant part - as they saw it - of the company's mainstream management structure. The role they gave Ian was brand new."

"So the CIO role became the executive in charge of Investing in Change."

"Yes. Although to start with, it was only for changes involving IT. A kind of natural next-generation role for an IT leader. But I heard that they expanded the scope fairly quickly afterwards, to cover all investments in change, whether or not they involved IT. Looking back, I'm sure that was their strategy all along."

"I get it. Makes sense. Anyway, with IT so pervasive to our businesses and lives, there can't be that many changes we could invest in that don't involve IT in some way. Actually, I don't think the role they gave Ian was quite as new as all that. When we want to know how our change projects are doing, we ask Lucy. She's got people who collect the data and turn it into Board reports. And she's the one who, with Howard, seems most interested in us doing Business Cases and Benefits Realization, if only for IT investments. All of that helps to explain why the four generations of CIO strategy are the ones that Ian showed me. Have you seen them?"

"No."

I stood up and walked over to my desk, found Ian's email, and sent the Four Generations picture to my printer. I picked it up, sat down again, and put it on the table between us. I left Simon to explore it while I carried on the conversation.

"It's ironic that one of Lucy's own Business Cases got me thinking about all this," I reflected. "Anyway, back to Ian's story. What did they do with Enterprise Architecture?"

Simon looked up from the Four Generations picture, and replied, "They put it in Corporate Strategy."

I started, "There's logic in that...", but Simon interrupted me before I could say any more. With the careless passion of a kneejerk reply, he said that he thought it was wrong, that he had told them so but they wouldn't listen. I held up my hand for him to stop.

"Stop. Enough drama. You're working in Corporate Strategy right now. So am I. So is Ian. The discipline, obviously, not the department. Wherever you put them in the organization, Enterprise Architecture and Investing in Change are essential aspects of corporate strategy. What we need next from you, Ivan, and Becky if we like her, is a Corporate Strategy for Enterprise Investment. As Ian and I already discussed, that means taking our existing strategy for Enterprise Architecture and merging it with the kind of strategy Ian leads and Becky knows all about. It'll be another opportunity for us all to raise our game."

I saw that I had provoked an emotional roadblock in Simon that he'd clung to from the past. We would find out, in time, whether he could let go. With that in mind, I decided to tell him what I wanted. "Let's have a strategy that gives people as much space and encouragement as possible, to create both the value and structure we want from the changes we invest in. I'm coming to the conclusion that in our current way of doing things, we've got too much friction, and of the wrong kind. We're making it harder, not easier, for people to deliver the most value they can from the investments we make." I watched him very carefully. He's a smart guy. But, I reckoned, he might not be tuned-in to my drift.

After a few moments he said, "By 'people', I expect you mean our company's customers, at least as much as our employees."

Much as I hate apologies, in my mind I apologized to Simon for underestimating him. That was exactly what I meant.

Observations

- Culture change demands skills that are very different from managing stable operations

- Projects are both implementations and investments. Implementation delivers the change (output); investment delivers the value (outcome)

- Is something a best practice because most people do it?

- Adapt portfolio theory for investments in change, and combine it with behavioral economics

- The CIO, or CTO, is often de facto the spokesperson for the enterprise's investments in change

- Enterprise Architecture and Investing in Change are essential aspects of corporate strategy.

FOUR

Lucy

Where to start? I had planned to talk to Lucy about her Business Case, but after the conversations with Ian and Simon, I was now concerned about the basic scope and value of her role. With IT so pervasive to everything, and with the four generations of CIO strategy in mind, was it time to do something different with my CTO? I decided to confront her directly, with that question. She and I go back quite a way, and she knows exactly what I'm like.

"There are a few things I need to talk through with you. For a start, why do we need a CTO?" I asked her. Her reply surprised me.

"I was waiting for you to ask me that."

"How come?"

"You met Ian Taylor. He has quite a reputation in the CIO and CTO community. I've done my research. I know his story."

"So?"

"When Ian stopped being a CIO, the company he worked for appointed a CTO who had previously been the Technology Services Manager. In what might seem a curious move, they put the CTO into Procurement. But, the twist in the tale is that Procurement no longer exists in that company, either. They moved the CTO into that function so that they could grow it into a fully-fledged Sourcing capability – for IT and everything else. In time, they let the Director of Procurement go, and elevated the CTO to become their first-ever Chief Officer for Sourcing. The ultimate result was that both the former CIO and former CTO ended up with very senior roles on the executive Board, but leading investments and sourcing, rather than information and technology."

"Do you want me to do the same?"

Lucy looked me in the eye, squinted and smiled. That was usually meant she was checking the angles before saying any more.

"Backtrack," she said, and reminded me that I had asked her why we needed a CTO before she told me about the Chief Officer for Sourcing. "What alternatives were you thinking of?"

I told her it had occurred to me, when listening to Simon talk about the CIO and CTO roles, that neither is actually what it says it is. As pseudo-Brands, they're confusing, to say the least.

"That Simon," she said, smiling. "To think that I gave him his job here in the first place."

I stayed quiet.

She continued, "Do I look after all the technologies the company uses? No. Do I want to? Is that what you were planning to ask me?"

"No. I was keeping an open mind. Remember, I asked you why we needed a CTO, not what role we should have instead."

"Do I have to answer now?"

"Answer when you're ready."

"Have we finished?"

"Actually, that wasn't what I really wanted to talk to you about. The CIO/CTO thing came up in conversation with Ian Taylor when we were discussing something else, and we shouldn't let it side-track us too much."

"I promise I will give you an answer. What was it you really wanted to talk to me about?"

I told her that I had been reading her Business Case in the bathtub, which made her laugh. She said next time that happened, I should phone her right there and then. I retorted, "It was nearly midnight," before realizing she was only flirting with me, as Lucy does with everyone. I

told her about the $87 million question and the
Statue of Liberty, and my confusion over how an
IT transformation could, in itself, deliver more
cash than it spent and therefore be NPV-positive.

"I know it's a lot of money," she said, which
surprised me, but I let her continue without
setting her straight. "That's because it's a global
transformation and we're a big company. You'll
have to ask Howard about the NPV," she said.
"He's the one that set it as the standard for
justifying projects, and his team did the
calculation for me."

"I'm asking you. It's your Business Case."

"Yes, but Howard endorsed it."

"Stop being evasive. It isn't helping. Is the
program you're proposing going to generate new
cash?"

"No."

"So why does your Business Case promise
that it will?"

"Because that's what we all have to promise
to get a Business Case approved."

"Right. That's what I thought. Does the
NPV help you make sure that the project delivers
as much value as possible, or that it has a better
probability of success?"

"No, I don't think so. And, anyway, we routinely ignore it once we get the go-ahead for investment."

"What about projects that do deliver new cash?"

"Those, too, as far as I've seen them."

"More pointless friction."

"What do you mean?"

"Friction in our culture and process for investing in change. Friction that stops us from getting the most value from investments, rather than making sure that we do."

"We've got to have some way of making sure we invest in the changes that are most worth doing. It can't just be a free-for-all."

"I'm not saying that it can be. Answer me this. Be brutally honest. All-in-all, what's the probability that we're getting the very best value from the changes we invest in?"

"Low."

"How low? Nought-33%, 33-66%, 66-100%"

With no hesitation, Lucy answered, "I'd guess nought-33%"

"Me, too. What about the probability that we're achieving the NPV shown in our Business Cases?"

"Roughly the same, or maybe less."

"And that we're achieving the actual benefits that people have in mind when proposing their projects, before they are converted into NPV?"

She looked more positive. "Probably a bit higher."

"As much as 50%?"

"If it's 50%, then I'd be pleasantly surprised."

"Very diplomatic. If it were you making the investment, which would you consider the best of the three options? Getting the most value, the NPV, or the business case benefits?"

"That's a complicated question."

"Because?"

"There are some projects where we absolutely need the specific benefits we're investing in. An example that comes to mind is to ensure legal or regulatory compliance."

"I agree. But, as long as we achieve that outcome, then there's nothing to stop us from driving the most value we can from whatever change the investment delivered."

"Except, maybe, the desire and determination to do so."

"Yes. Well said. Call it enterprise."

Lucy continued, "For projects with direct cash benefits, we would want to achieve the NPV. But your challenge still applies. Why not also get as much value from those projects as we can, financial or otherwise?"

"Indeed. And, what about your transformation program? Which of the three types of outcome should we most drive it to achieve? Maximum value, NPV, or the Business Case benefits?"

Lucy, who is usually very sure of keeping and using eye contact, looked over my shoulder. I gave her a second or two and then asked what was troubling her. "I feel I have to tell a terrible truth," she said, carefully, looking me in the eye again.

"Tell me."

"I don't think the IT transformation program is like that."

She stopped again, and then continued.

"It's an architectural transformation, to better position us for the future. That's the reason I think we need to do it."

"Thank you for leveling with me. Let me check if I've understood you properly. Your program is about architectural change, not delivering specific benefits. It will be NPV-negative. But, we might be able to drive value from whatever it delivers, in ways we may not know until we get to the end."

"Yes."

"So wouldn't it be better, more transparent, and more prudent if your proposal said that?"

"In theory, it would. But then we wouldn't invest in it."

"Why not?"

"I see where you're taking this. But will Howard agree?"

"That's why I just said 'transparent' and 'prudent'. I was trying them out on you first. I'm talking to Howard next."

Lucy reminded me that I'd said there were a few things I wanted to talk through with her. She asked if there was anything else.

"Oh, yes. Consumerization. Of the IT market."

"What about it?"

"What's the impact on all of this?"

"I'm not sure what you're asking me."

"Tell me how the consumerization of the IT market has impacted our investments in change — your IT transformation program, for example."

"Consumerization is one of the main drivers for the investment I've proposed. We need to transform our worldwide IT infrastructure so that people can use their own consumer technologies."

I asked Lucy which people she was referring to.

"Our employees," she replied, looking puzzled by my question. Thinking back to my conversation with Ian, perhaps my CTO was indeed a generation behind the market.

"And why is that worth $87 million to us?"

I could see she didn't have an answer, so I gave her something to take away and think about.

"If you were to focus on our customers, as well as our employees, I expect your program could be quite different."

Finally, I asked Lucy whether she wanted to discuss again the idea of becoming our global Chief Officer for Sourcing. She said that she did, but not right then.

"Good luck with Howard," she said.

"You know me better than that, Lucy. With things like this, luck doesn't come into it."

Observations

- In some investment cultures, once an investment is approved the proposed value gets ignored

- Even in projects where we need the specific benefits we've invested in (e.g. compliance), the aim is to deliver as much value as possible

- Architectural transformations are about investing in the delivery of structure, not value

- People often find out the value they can create from an investment only when the change has been delivered

- The consumerization of the IT market has changed the landscape for investing in change.

FIVE

Howard

Howard has been with the company ten years longer than I have. He was Financial Controller before my predecessor promoted him to CFO, about the same time as I was recruited as CMO. So we used to be peers, now he works for me.

On a personal level, we both love rock music, especially from the 1970s. With his wife and mine, we've often made a foursome at some concerts by the greatest. Howard also plays a mean electric guitar.

Before my appointment as CEO, the corporate strategy had been focused on increasing profits through efficiencies. Given that the world economy was collapsing at the time, we all agreed with that strategy, and it probably saved the company. But, there came a time when the main Board decided, on behalf of the investors, that we needed a new strategy based on productivity and revenue growth. That's one reason I got the job I have today. When I look at Howard, I think I see signs that he preferred the previous corporate strategy to the one I'm now leading, but I know that my own prejudices could be coloring my judgment.

I called on Howard in his office, and said I wanted to talk about Lucy's Business Case. But first, I said, I needed to explore with him something about our investments, in general. I asked him to tell me the total positive cash flow our change projects had generated in the last financial year. The question took him by surprise, which is what I'd anticipated. I told him that it could be gross or net, whichever he preferred.

When Howard isn't ready to talk, he expresses himself with his hands. He looked at me over the top of his spectacles, held both hands in front of him, and tapped the opposing fingers on each other. Then he switched to alternately tapping the palm of one hand on the back of the other. Finally, he dropped both hands palms-down onto his desk and said, as assertively as he could muster, "We don't have those numbers available right now."

"OK."

"Why do you want to know?"

"I've been thinking about our investments in change."

"What about them?"

"Whether we're encouraging everyone to exploit them as much as possible, to deliver the most value they can. Whether, all-in-all, they are the most risk-efficient way of achieving our goals."

"I'm sure we could always do better. Why the question about cash?"

"Because we're choosing projects based on the NPV that they promise. Only ones with positive NPVs get approved, so I wondered how much of that cash we actually see."

He explained that in many cases it was a theoretical calculation, so that all projects could be compared on a level playing field. We could use other financial appraisal methods such as Internal Rate of Return (IRR), or Cost-Benefit Analysis (CBA), but NPV was the one we had agreed upon.

I told him that I thought it might be better if we used none of those methods. He looked at me as if I had gone mad.

"You're looking at me as if I've gone mad," I said.

"I just can't believe what I'm hearing. You want to remove the controls we have on capital spending."

"No, I want to replace the criteria we use to choose our investments, with better ones. I don't think the criteria we use are working to our advantage. If anything, it's the opposite. And, I don't think it should matter whether the investment includes capex[3] or not. Whatever controls we have need to be for all our investments in change. I don't think we're at greater risk of a change destroying more value than it's worth, just because the investment includes capex."

In an unconvinced tone of voice, he asked, "What do you propose instead?"

"Complete transparency of the main reason for investing, and all the costs. Plus the probability of success. All based on the principle of prudence, of course."

"Do you have an example of a 'reason for investing'?"

"Sure. Legal or regulatory compliance."

"You mean a mandatory project."

"No such thing. We could always choose not to do it."

---

[3] Capex: Capital Expenditure.

"But we could go to jail."

"I know. That's why it's worth choosing wisely. But, to get back to the point, the only value of a compliance project is that we are compliant. That is, quite clearly, what we want the investment to deliver. A simple, authoritative, yes or no. It's NPV-negative, but I agree with you we'll do it anyway. It makes the company no more valuable than we already were, so the more economical the investment, the better. Here's another one. Brand reputation. No new cash flow, NPV-negative, but from time-to-time we'll invest in that too. Then, there are the investments we make in our architecture, to ensure we are in good shape for the future..."

I could tell he had gotten the point, and I didn't push it any further. It wasn't the conversation I wanted to have with him, but it had paved the way.

"I'll cut to the punch line," I said, "I think we're failing to make the most of our investments in change, despite all the controls we've put in place. As far as I can tell, we're stifling people's innovation and enterprise, rather than encouraging them. I am going to appoint a Chief Officer, to remove the unproductive friction from our investment process, and to take Board-level accountability for our performance in delivering value from change."

"You've caught me by surprise with all of this. How long have you been planning it?"

I told him that I hadn't been planning it at all, but that it had rapidly become clear to me that there could be a better way of doing things. "We're on a journey of discovery together. Jamming, strategically, if you like. Are you in?"

"Sure, count me in. But it's very different from what I was taught about capital planning and investment."

"That's interesting. Very interesting. Have you ever heard of the Project Probability Paradox?"

"No. What's that?"

So I explained to Howard what Ian Taylor had told me, about cultures where the higher the probability of a project being approved, the lower its probability of success. He said he'd like to reflect on that.

I asked him how he felt about our conversation, in general. Expressive hands again, while he considered his answer. Then, he said he was bothered by the implications. I was carefully silent, while he pieced together the best way to say what those implications were.

"It's what the changes you're talking about will effectively say about the financial controls we've been applying to our investments. And therefore about Finance."

"Finance, as in your department?"

"Yes. And throughout the company."

"I understand. But surely everyone knows that Finance isn't the same as Investment? I'm certain we need to apply rigorous financial controls to the monetary aspects of investing in change. We don't want to waste a cent. But, the further I get into this subject, the more I realize that we have a gap in our senior management structure. I think that between Finance and IT you've been trying to fill that gap. That's certainly prevented a free-for-all, but it's also meant that the gap was harder to see."

This time, when Howard fell silent, he stayed perfectly still. No hands. I don't think he even blinked, until he said, "What gap?"

"Enterprise Investment."

"Never heard of it."

"It's a combination of Enterprise Architecture and Investing in Change."

"Oh."

"We're good at Enterprise Architecture, and getting better all the time. The other day I met someone who Simon knows from his past, who specializes in strategies for Investing in Change. Frankly, I don't think we're anywhere near as good at that as we could be. And he, Simon's friend, floated the idea with me of putting the two together into a single strategy. Enterprise Architecture plus Investing in Change equals Enterprise Investment."

Howard asked me what the advantage was of combining Enterprise Architecture and Investing in Change.

I replied, "We need the changes we invest in to deliver, collectively, and efficiently, both the value and structure we want. As separate capabilities, Enterprise Architecture is focused on the delivery of structure, and Investing in Change on the delivery of value. I expect we would retain some distinct capabilities in each, but at a Board level would have one strategy, one portfolio, and one Chief Officer."

"Do you want to keep some distinction between them because of creative tensions?"

"Yes. And because they are, quite simply, very different capabilities."

"OK. Do you have someone in mind as the Chief Officer?"

"Possibly. But I'm not ready to say anything yet."

"I understand."

"Thank you," I said. "There's one other thing I just want to check. In Lucy's Business Case for her $87 million IT Transformation Program, who calculated the Net Present Value?"

"We did."

"We?"

"Finance."

"Doesn't that give you a conflict of interest when it comes to our decision to approve or reject the proposal? Treat that as a rhetorical question if you like."

"No. It's OK. I can see what you mean. People often find those calculations a bit abstract. We were only trying to help."

Observations

- In an investment strategy founded on NPV, the amount of cash actually delivered by the portfolio is the key measure of success

- A project isn't likely to be at risk of destroying more value than it's worth, just because the investment includes capex

- Investments that are protecting the existing value of the company - not growing its value - need to be as economical as possible

- There's a conflict of interest between judging the potential value of an investment, and helping to produce the proposal

- The person who will deliver the value of an investment must be the one accountable for the proposal.

SIX

Ivan

There was something about that last thing Howard had said, about "only trying to help", that niggled me. Something I had read somewhere. But, I couldn't put my finger on where that was, or why I was bothered.

Between the conversation with Howard about Enterprise Investment and my next one, with Ivan, a whole week passed in which I needed to get back to my day job. That included spending an entire day on our Brand strategy, which is - in business - as close to my heart as you can get. Annoyingly, it was facilitated by an external consultant who hadn't done his homework. He didn't to seem to know my background or the work we had done on Experiences-Oriented Architecture, which I will tell you about in a moment. As a result, he made some fundamental errors. As well as talking down to me, he concentrated far too much on marketing, and not nearly enough on the coherency with which we appear in our customers' experiences. I came close to ending the workshop at lunchtime. But, we kept going, and some useful output emerged. I told my Chief Marketing Officer never to let that facilitator near me again.

Ivan Bingham was one of our Enterprise Architects. In fact, the best I've ever known. We plucked Ivan out of our Canadian subsidiary, where he was working in the IT department. We got him designing an idea Simon had, in Japan, just after joining the company. For a while, Ivan didn't seem to know where to start. But, once he got going, and with permission to express himself, he produced a brilliantly simple and innovative design.

Simon's idea was to get the benefits of sharing services across our businesses, without creating a Shared Services organization. There's a big difference, both structurally and culturally, between our businesses sharing services, and having a Shared Services unit.

The original design concept was called 'virtual hubs'. It became a key part of our Experiences-Oriented, Virtual Enterprise architecture, which we modeled like this[4]:

---

[4] See RecrEAtion

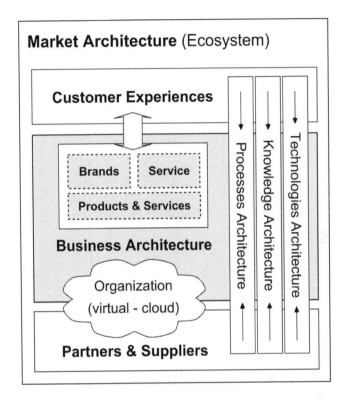

Enterprise Architecture:
Experiences-Oriented Virtual Enterprise

The basic premise of this architecture is that a market will work whether or not our enterprise exists. We have to decide what we bring to the party. Our value comes from how well we appear in our Customer's experiences, through the market's processes, knowledge, and technologies. Behind the scenes, we can organize ourselves as we like, with employees, partners and suppliers, financial structures, and so on. As far as Customers are concerned, our organization is a 'cloud'. For all they know, we might not even exist.

So, as you can see, instead of 'virtual hubs' we decided to create a 'cloud organization'. Once we had made that decision, each time we heard or read about 'cloud computing' we smiled to ourselves. We had borrowed the IT industry's design concept, and blown it up into something much more powerful and valuable!

Ivan took this idea and turned it from 'vaporware' into a design we could invest in and exploit. With Human Resources specialists, and people in our local businesses, he created 'Capability Networks' around the world. Each of these includes both our own employees and key individuals from our partners and suppliers. It was interesting to see that some of our people were still locked in to old-school organizational thinking, reluctant to include externals in their networks. We suggested they think of them as 'session musicians'. Specialists who can add-to and enhance our performance, without being permanent members of the band.

Now, people who represent the same capability in different businesses share and maintain knowledge of each other's strengths and areas of expertise. On a quid-pro-quo basis, they routinely assist each other in achieving the best, quickest, and most productive outcome for their local colleagues. In effect, if you are working with one of them, you are actually working with all of them. Each of our businesses has on-demand access to capabilities way beyond their local scale.

So far, we had built a Finance network, a Marketing network, a Corporate Communications network, and - of course - an Enterprise Architecture network. Everyone liked the fact that our employees still worked for a local business rather than some remote shared-services unit. It also enhanced empathy, collaboration, and mutual value-creation between businesses in ways that we don't think a Shared Services organization ever can. Also, by keeping the internal sharing on a quid-pro-quo basis as much as possible, we managed to avoid all the distractions that come with 'cross-charging' costs between budgets, apart from when the numbers involved are exceptionally large. Some fans of Shared Services organizations argued that our Capability Networks were less efficient. They might be right, depending on which unit cost ratios are used to measure efficiency. We consider any such loss in efficiency to be an investment worth making.

Next on Ivan's roll-out plan was a Sourcing network, so my conversation with Lucy had been very timely. Now, I was wondering whether we should also build an Investing in Change network, or redesign the Enterprise Architecture network as Enterprise Investment.

I summarized for Ivan my journey so far, from the bathtub, via Ian Taylor, Simon, Becky Chekhova, and Lucy, to the conversation with Howard. When I mentioned Becky's apparent reaction to having an Enterprise Architect involved, I watched him very closely. A brief look crossed his face which seemed to say, "Here we go again."

Then, I asked Ivan whether he thought we should create a new Capability Network for Investing in Change, or redesign the one we already had for Enterprise Architecture.

Rather than answer, he started with a question. "What's the objective?"

"Great question! Tell me what you think it is."

"Enhancing the performance of our investments in change. Where 'performance' means both the value and structure they produce, and how efficiently they produce them."

"Agreed," I said.

"OK," Ivan continued. "As shorthand, I'm going to call Enterprise Architecture 'EA', and Investing in change 'IC'. So the design question we are considering is whether we would best achieve the objective we've agreed with EA and IC as separate Capability Networks, or as a combined one."

"Indeed. We would call the combined capability Enterprise Investment."

"Shorthand, 'EI'."

"Yes."

"I'll make an observation, which I think might help."

"Go on."

"All the Capability Networks we've built to date are represented by a Chief Officer, both for the Corporation and in each of our Business Units - except one."

"Enterprise Architecture."

"Do you think EA will ever have a dedicated C-level executive?"

"No. SVP is about as senior as I expect it will get."

"What about Investing in Change? Would that have a Chief Officer?"

"That's interesting, because Ian Taylor is currently one of those, but he's the person that told me it would be better to combine EA and IC. I think he knows his own role is currently incomplete, because it's missing EA. I remember, when Simon was telling me what happened to Ian, he said that the CEO and Strategy Director put EA into the Corporate Strategy department, rather than combine it with Investing in Change."

Ivan frowned. "So, Ian didn't put it there?"

"No."

"Did Simon indicate whether he thought that was the right answer?"

"You can say that again. When I told him it sounded like the logical thing to do, he nearly exploded. I had to explain that I meant making sure EA is a corporate strategy discipline, not necessarily putting it in a Corporate Strategy department."

"I've never seen Simon explode. He must believe, passionately, that Ian's CEO made the wrong choice. And, I happen to think that Simon is a genius. I wouldn't be here now, but for the ideas he's had, and the leadership he's given me."

I agreed with Ivan about Simon. But, the way Simon had reacted to my observation about EA and Corporate Strategy had stopped me pursuing the subject with him. I said it would be good to know why Ian's former CEO had given him Investing in Change, but taken away Enterprise Architecture. Ivan suggested we gave her a call.

"No, let's ask Ian himself," I said. "Get Trudy to set up a conference call, if Ian's willing. I've a feeling we should find out what he says, before deciding what to do next."

"OK," said Ivan, and left my office to see Trudy.

A couple of hours later, Trudy told me that Ian had agreed to our conference call, but we would have to wait a week before talking to him.

Meanwhile, there were much more important matters to deal with. Worst, we got some terrible news from our South African business. An accident at one of our plants there killed 26 of our employees, and injured over 100 more. They were the first fatalities we'd had, anywhere in the world, for over 20 years. Some of our businesses are in dangerous industries. We invest a lot in safety. I've had people try and persuade me that the primary motive for investing in safety is to protect our reputation. They are wrong. It is to protect our people and their families, and everyone who lives in the communities where we operate. I spent a long twenty-fours without sleep, on the phone to our local managers, watching the live news feeds, and being interviewed by journalists. Of course, I followed our stock price, that's my job too. It fell a little, but nothing we couldn't recover in time. Our priorities were to ensure that the site in South Africa was made safe, to look after the families of the people who had died, and to care for the people who were injured.

I took guidance on how soon to fly to South Africa from our local Managing Director, and from Wendy Martin, my Chief Officer for Communications. It's a hard one to judge, and we've seen people in my kind of position get it very wrong. At the end of the first twenty-four hours after the accident, I flew over to join the local efforts in person. I slept on the plane to Johannesburg, spent the next 36 hours working non-stop with our excellent local leadership and some of our other people who'd flown in from around the world, then slept on the plane back to New York. If you'll permit me a little levity in such a serious moment, considering Business Cases for IT transformations in the bathtub at midnight is trivial, compared with what it can really take to be a CEO.

Two days after I returned from South Africa, Becky Chekhova arrived in town. The same day, Ivan and I also talked to Ian Taylor on speakerphone in my office.

"Hello," Ian began, "I'm sorry about the situation in South Africa."

"Thank you," I replied. "Our colleagues down there are handling it the very best anyone could under the circumstances. It's a difficult moment for the families and friends of the people who died, and for the many people who are injured."

"Sure." Ian left a short silence, before asking, "I expect you want to talk to me about Enterprise Investment again. How can I help?"

I nodded to Ivan, to lead the conversation. "Hello Ian, this is Ivan Bingham. I'm one of Michael's Enterprise Architects. It's a privilege to talk to you. Michael and I were exploring whether to treat Enterprise Architecture and Investing in Change as separate capabilities, or merge them into one."

"OK."

"We need to ask you a question about your own history and experiences."

"I'll tell you what I can."

"When you stopped being a CIO and were given a Chief Officer role for Investing in Change, we understand that this didn't include EA. Is that correct?"

"You've done your homework. Yes, that's correct."

"Why not?"

"Three reasons. First, EA was not a significant force in the company, so what happened to it was not considered vital. Second, I think the company's Strategy Director wanted to - shall we say - 'play' with EA to see what he could do with it. And, third, I took my eye off the ball. I was too busy trying to figure out the strategy for Investing in Change to think about what might happen to EA."

"Thank you," Ivan said. "To pick up the first of those reasons, and as I expect you know, EA is already a significant force in our company. How much of a difference do you think that should make in our decision whether to combine it with Investing in Change?"

"I think they should be combined anyway."

Ivan asked, "Why haven't you done it yet?"

"Because I didn't think of it until a couple of years ago, when I was having dinner in London with Simon. The company I'm currently working for has no formalized EA at all, so there's nothing to combine. For now, we're still up to our eyeballs in the practicalities and politics of sorting out the portfolio of investments in change."

I asked Ian, "Won't you miss Becky, then, if she moves back over here?"

"Yes, but she's ready to go back to America. She's been mentoring someone from the company's Finance community to replace her,"

"That sounds a bit risky," I said, "do they get the differences between Finance and Investment?"

"They're getting there. She's a good mentor."

Ivan asked, "Did you choose someone from Finance on purpose, to embody the differences through their change in values and behaviors?"

"Yes. It's risky. But a strategy that I'm confident will work."

I asked, "What's the probability of success?"

"I like your question, Michael. Right now, medium, I'd say. So we are paying a lot of attention, all the time, to what might cause it to fail."

It occurred to me that Ian was running the conversation, even though Ivan and I were asking the questions.

I said, "Ian, we have to go shortly. Thank you for taking the time to talk to us. Please tell us if there is anything we can do for you in return."

"Can we talk again in a month's time? You know, I'm very interested in what you're doing over there. I think it will be very enlightening."

"Yes, of course," I replied, smiling at his careful reference to our dinner conversation about music. "Please talk to Trudy about reserving some time."

"Thank you. I'm looking forward to it already."

"Great. Talk to you soon."

We ended the call. I suggested to Ivan that we get a cup of coffee each, and talk through what we had learned. He asked if he should get Trudy to bring us the coffees. I told him it would be good for us to take a break, and a walk, and get them ourselves.

"I'll tell you what I'm thinking," I said, as we sat back down at the meeting table in my office. "I need to connect these conversations back to reality. Right now, there's something a bit abstract about it all. Maybe I'm a bit tired from the events in South Africa. I do believe there is something important in all of this for the success of our enterprise, otherwise you wouldn't find me spending all this time on it. However, at the moment, there's a small, but growing, part of me that is telling me not to bother."

Ivan is an intelligent guy who knows me well. I was being candid, and gently provocative. He didn't say anything for a few moments and drank some coffee while he considered how best to respond.

"Before South Africa happened," he said, "we agreed on an objective for Enterprise Investment. As long as we are still happy with that objective, let's make it drive the conversation."

"Yes," I agreed.

"I wrote it down. Actually, I didn't. I made a note of it on my phone. I'm showing my age." That made me smile, as Ivan was only thirty-four.

"What was it?" I thought I knew anyway, but I hadn't noted it down. Ivan took his phone out his pocket and after a few seconds found his note.

"Here it is. Enhancing the performance of our investments in change. Where 'performance' means both the value and structure they produce, and how efficiently they produce them."

"Indeed."

"So, what would connect back to reality all of the conversations that have happened, so far?"

"Well, the objective does, for a start. Now, I'm starting to envisage people producing value from the changes we invest in, in ways they couldn't otherwise do. I can see people making those changes happen as efficiently as possible. I can also see executives deciding differently from today which changes to invest in. And, I can sort-of perceive a structure in which all of that happens. It's not a physical structure, of course."

"What kind of structure are you thinking of?"

"Well, it's tempting to think of an organizational structure, but there's a problem with that. Many of the people who are producing value from our investments are outside our organization: Customers, investors, partners, suppliers, and so on. They are participating in our enterprise, but not part of our organization."

"And, I guess, we're participating in whatever they're doing, too."

"No need to guess. That's how business has always worked."

"And, that's why the market is an ecosystem in our architecture model."

"Yes."

"Then, the changes we invest in are altering the ecosystem, or at least attempting to."

"That's right. Now what if the ecosystem doesn't want to be changed?"

"Well, either it will manage to stop the change, or - if it can't - will neutralize its effects."

"Hmm." I had made a connection between the conversation Ivan and I were having and the Investment Culture Diagnosis that Ian Taylor had worked through with me. The true implications of what that one page was telling us were only just beginning to emerge. It highlighted how the mini-ecosystem of our own organization currently behaved towards investments in change. For us to achieve the objective that Ivan and I had discussed, we would need some of those behaviors to change. To echo my question of Ivan, I thought, "What if the ecosystem didn't want to be changed?"

Ivan, as if reading my mind, said, "Antibodies," cryptically.

"What?"

"That's what I've heard people who are agents of change call the people who resist change. Antibodies."

"Like in a living organism?"

"Yes."

"But, isn't the purpose of antibodies to prevent the organism from harmful infections?"

"I think so. Something like that."

"Agents of stability, if you like, versus agents of undesirable change."

"That's an interesting way of describing it. Mind you, antibodies can also resist desirable change."

"Agents of stability. Agents of change. Something's starting to form in my mind."

Ivan carefully stayed quiet while I collected my thoughts. When I was ready, I took a piece of paper and drew a picture as I talked. Here's what I said, followed by the picture that I drew.

"OK. Here's our enterprise." I drew a box on the paper. "To be successful in our strategy for creating value and structure, we have to invest in both stability and change. We get value and structure from stability, plus value and structure from change. The combination of value and structure from stability and change needs to come to the overall value and structure that we want. Stability has its agents, and so does change. There's an essential contest between them, which is useful to our strategy as long as we know how to harness it."

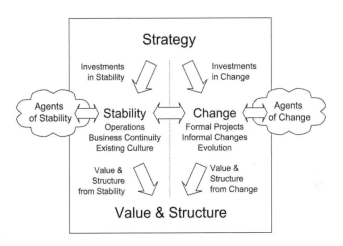

I continued, "Some of our people are bound to be agents of value from either stability or change, because of the roles that they have. Overall, we need our corporate culture to be about creating value from the best balance of both. At last some pieces are beginning to fall into place."

"What pieces? Help me."

I noticed that Ivan was acting as facilitator now, which was fine with me for the moment.

I continued, "Up to now, most of the conversations have tended to focus on structural questions. Should we combine Enterprise Architecture with Investing in Change? What's the future role of a CIO or CTO? Is it best to choose investments using NPV or something else?

What questions should a Business Case or Investment Proposal contain, and in which order? And so on. I should have taken more notice of Ian's title for his one-pager. It's an Investment Culture Diagnosis, not Investment Structure Diagnosis."

"So, if I have understood you right, we need to be talking about how, in reality rather than in theory, we influence the culture of our ecosystem in ways that achieve the objective that you and I agreed on. Does that mean we should stop looking at how we might redesign the structure?"

"No, I think structure has a vital impact on culture. But it is unlikely to change the culture on its own. Depending on how much value our ecosystem places on formalized structure, it may change things a lot, or very little."

Ivan then voiced what I was also thinking. "That means, achieving the objective you and I agreed on would be a significant challenge, strategically."

"Yes, Ivan, it would. Are you up for it?"

He looked at the table briefly, then locked eye contact with me. "You bet."

"Good. I'm back in. That was a tricky conversation. Thank you for guiding us through. Let's leave it there until we've met Becky."

Observations

- The basic premise in modeling and designing an enterprise is that it doesn't have to exist for a market to work

- An enterprise creates value through its appearances in customers' experiences

- To share services across an enterprise, Capability Networks are a cultural and structural alternative to having a Shared Services organization

- The changes we invest in are attempts to change the ecosystem

- Ecosystems can resist change, both harmful and desirable

- There's an essential contest between stability and change, and the agents of each

- The extent to which structure impacts culture depends on how much value the ecosystem places on formalized structures.

SEVEN

Becky

Simon had been right about Becky, when he said after our video call that some people could find her intimidating. Don't get me wrong. There is nothing unpleasant about the way she handles people - quite the opposite. She is assertive, not aggressive.

Some people will find her intimidating because she is perfectly in charge of her emotions. Whatever others might have in mind for her, she feels only what she chooses to feel.

For our dinner with Becky, Trudy had chosen a Michelin-starred restaurant on the Brooklyn waterfront, with a view over the East River towards Lower Manhattan. It was a nice touch for someone from Wall Street who wanted to come home.

We had arranged to meet Becky at the restaurant, so I had a few minutes in the cab with Simon and Ivan. I told them what we needed to find out. Then, I asked Ivan to summarize for Simon our thoughts about ecosystems, culture, and structure. I said that I wanted us to assume Becky was technically proficient, and focus on what impact we thought she might have on our people's behaviors towards investments in change. I also told Ivan to probe for any hostility towards Enterprise Architects.

Trudy had secured us the restaurant's best table, by the window, and Becky was already sitting there when the three of us walked in. As we approached her she stood up, said to Simon and me that it was good to see us again, and then I introduced her to Ivan.

She said to me, "Thank you for choosing this restaurant, and this view."

I replied, "It was all Trudy's doing, but I'm glad that you like it."

We all sat down. Simon and Ivan respected my preference to wait until dessert before talking business. Becky just went with the flow. We spent the next two hours talking about New York and London, the state of the global economy, what we thought America needed to do next, and how this played out given the nation's history and its culture.

As dessert arrived I looked at Simon in the way that he knows it's time to talk shop.

He began, "Becky, the last time we spoke you talked about two options for changing our investment culture. Now that we're all here together, we'd like to hear more."

"Sure, Simon. So, option one is to change the investment culture as an integral part of other changes you're making. Option two is to target the investment culture directly. I remember telling you than the first is usually easier, but less overt."

"Indeed," replied Simon. "A big culture change has been Michael's focus on productivity, rather than efficiency. Also, we've been developing an explicit management focus on our structural performance, and on structural innovations. Our management teams around the world have been on a journey to integrate formalized Enterprise Architecture into their strategies, business plans, and change projects. We had to, in effect, re-create Enterprise Architecture to make all that possible."

As Simon kept talking, Ivan and I were studying Becky for any visible reactions to the repeated mention of Enterprise Architecture. There were none. Instead, she said, "Ian told me what you've achieved with EA. He said it was remarkable, and for the work that he and I have been doing, the missing part of the jigsaw. We have focused people on the value they get from their portfolio of investments in change. You've focused them on the structure they get and how that structure performs. Now, we just have to put those two outcomes together."

Simon decided to be very direct. "When you, Michael, and I spoke before, and we mentioned Ivan might join us for dinner, we were concerned about your apparent reaction. It looked to us like you have a problem with Enterprise Architects."

Becky was equally direct in her response. "I know. I wanted you to see that."

"Why?"

"Because I've met some people with that title who don't seem to know that they work on behalf of the investors. Of course, the good ones know that."

"Who do the others seem to think they work for?"

"Some of them, for the delivery people. Some don't seem to know. A few - kinda abstractly - for Enterprise Architecture itself, or even a particular way of doing it." As she finished, she turned to look at Ivan. Simon and I did the same.

Ivan knew it was time for him to talk. Although he was sitting down, I noticed he spoke as if standing up.

"Let's see if this helps," he started. "I'm interested in designing changes to our enterprise's structure that achieve specific performance outcomes. Together with Michael, Simon, and our colleagues around the world, we regularly review whether the enterprise's structural performance is - over time - improving or decaying, using a number of key ratios. They are the same kinds of ratio that external investors use to judge the probability of our enterprise contributing to their goals in the future. We invest in structural innovations that enhance those performance ratios. We have a worldwide community of enterprise architects - small e, small a - that includes, for example, many of our business executives, as well as people actually called Enterprise Architect - capital E, capital A. It's one of our Capability Networks, as we call them. Since Simon started us on this journey, we've become much, much better at designing and investing in structure. But, our structural performance drives only some of the changes we invest in. Our problem is that we are lacking the capability to create as much value as possible from all the projects we do, structural or not. No, let me correct that. Thanks to Ian Taylor's unscripted appearance in our journey here, we now know that, while our structure is lacking capability, our main problem may well be that our culture is lacking enterprise. If anything, our structure is stifling our culture, with too much of the wrong kind of friction."

Nobody said anything, for a few moments. Then before any of us at the table could speak, a waiter appeared and asked, "Will there be anything else?" Without looking at him, I held up my hand to indicate that he should come back in five minutes.

Becky replied to Ivan with a nod that communicated respect, and then asked me, "Do you have any time tomorrow? I'd like to tell you what I'm thinking, and the office will be better than here."

"You must work for Ian Taylor," I said, light-heartedly. "He and I had dinner, then met in the office the next day. Did he teach you that one?"

"The other way around. I taught him."

I took my phone out of my jacket, and checked my schedule. "I can give you an hour at 4 P.M. I suggest you spend as much time tomorrow as you can with these two gentlemen, then come and see me at four. Just you."

On either side of me, Simon and Ivan were also checking their schedules. "Move everything you can," I told them. "I'm beginning to get

excited about all of this. I've just raised the
priority."

Later, as we all got up to leave the
restaurant, Ivan said to me quietly, "So you
decided to bother, after all."

I gave him a sideways smile in return.

Becky came to my office promptly at 4 P.M.
the next day. I said, "We have more than an hour,
if we want. I've cleared my evening schedule."

"Thank you."

I asked her how the guys had been.

"Impressive."

"Yes, they are. So, what have you got for
me?"

"A problem."

So, I wasn't the only one who could be
provocative. I was certain she knew I would balk
at that response. I decided to smile at her, stay
quiet, and find out what came next.

She continued, "The problem here is the
same as in many other enterprises. Ivan told me
about the objective you agreed on, about

enhancing the performance of your investments in change. Hard to argue with that. But, as far as the guys could tell me, you have no idea what your performance currently is. The only metrics you have are for projects involving IT. Even they are mainly about implementation performance, rather than investment. So, here's your problem. People like me work on probabilities. I'd like to know what the probability currently is that your enterprise will deliver both the value and structure you need from your portfolio of investments in change. Then, beyond that, there's the probability of delivering the most value you can – not just the value you need. Apart from gut feel, you don't know what those probabilities are."

Becky stopped again, to see if I reacted. I didn't.

"Now, I'm convinced we can solve that problem, and in doing so achieve the objective you've set. For me, that's vital. As much as I want to move back to New York, if I didn't think I could win here, I wouldn't be prepared to invest myself in your strategy. I'd thank you for your time and walk away now."

It was, I decided, my turn to speak.

"Becky," I said, raising my voice a little, "If you want to work for me, never do that again."

"If you're talking about my tactic of hitting you with a problem, I won't. I decided to risk it just this once."

"OK. I agree that we have the problem. We don't know our current performance at creating value from change."

"Right. Let's talk about achieving your objective. I'd like to start with something Simon drew with your people in Abu Dhabi. He said that when he started here, you sent him on a world tour, and this came up near the end."

"That's true. I wanted him to experience our enterprise and architecture first hand, and to meet some of our influential leaders out there. What did he show you?"

Becky put a piece of paper on the table between us, and lay a pen down next to it. "I think this is a very important picture, although the version on the table - the original - isn't quite right. We've been using it today to explore what's wrong with it, why, and what to change."

This is the picture that Becky was describing. It maps various capabilities onto an end-to-end process for investing in change, to show where they make the most contribution, and therefore can have the most influence:

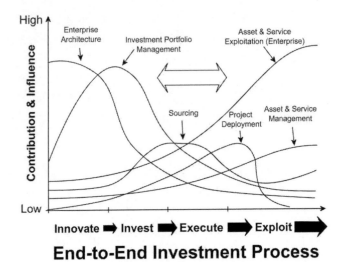

End-to-End Investment Process

"Do you want me to talk you through it?" she asked.

"No," I replied, "I've seen it before. Just tell me what's wrong with it."

"Two details. It underestimates the contribution of Sourcing, and suggests that Projects are only about deployment."

I looked again at the picture. I agreed with Becky's first point, and connected it with my conversation with Lucy about Sourcing. I also remembered saying to Ian Taylor that we managed projects as implementations rather than investments, and telling Simon that it's the investment that delivers value, while the implementation delivers change.

I said to Becky, "I agree with you on both counts. Why, do you think we got those details wrong?"

"Because it was drawn to answer a different question. Simon was exploring the contribution of Enterprise Architecture."

"OK, I can accept that. So how should it look?"

Becky put a second version of the picture on the table:

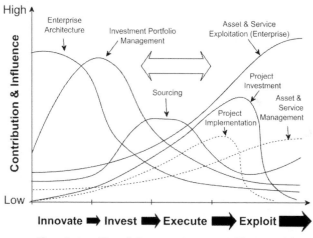

End-to-End Investment Process
(Amended)

I explored this version out loud, finishing with a question. "So, the Sourcing contribution is now higher; I think it should be higher still. You've added the Project Investment capability. You've also made another change you didn't mention. Project Implementation, and Asset & Service Management, are now dotted lines. Why?"

"Because we have the option to source those both internally and externally. Your 'cloud organization' makes that more obvious, easier, and more likely to succeed. The others are all core capabilities. The essence of being an enterprise."

Becky would have noticed me being silent for a second. I was thinking about 'antibodies' and the conversation with Ivan. There were plenty of people in our company, all around the world, who would regard as core capabilities the two things that the amended picture showed as optional. I said to Becky, "I was quiet there for a moment as I was linking what you said to a conversation I had with Ivan about ecosystems, antibodies, and culture."

"Sure, he told me about it."

"Right. Let's move on. It's becoming clear to me that I may well need to start our culture change with the executive Board. We're missing two Chief Officer roles and the strategies they would be leading."

"Yes, you are."

"Is that the only way to achieve the result we're looking for? By starting with the executives?"

"No. You can achieve it by starting bottom-up or middle-outwards. That's a question of strategy. But, one way or another, you will end up changing the Board."

"Give me an example of middle-outwards."

"Setting up an Investment Management Office, an IMO. Making sure people see how different it is from a Program Management Office, or PMO. Without a Chief Officer for Enterprise Investment, the IMO would need to work for you directly."

"OK. That's another option. Everything we talk about is in confidence, right?"

Becky nodded, looking faintly offended.

I continued, "I was already thinking of making Simon our Chief Officer for Enterprise Investment. I have also started talking to our CTO about becoming the Chief Officer for Sourcing."

"Those are, ultimately, the two new roles you'll need."

"If I can arrange it, would you like to join us? We will need an SVP of Investing in Change. Ivan would most likely take over from Simon as our SVP of Enterprise Architecture."

"Yes, I would."

"Excellent. Let me talk it through with our SVP of Human Resources."

"Thank you. Is there anything I can provide you with?"

"Your resume."

"It will be in your inbox this evening."

"Good. When is your flight home?"

I noticed she carefully changed the question before answering it. "My original flight back to London was first thing this morning. I'm now booked on one later tonight. I'm giving a Board presentation tomorrow afternoon."

"Do a good one."

"Say again?"

"Around here, we never wish each other 'good luck'. We say, 'Do a good one'. It's more inspiring."

She smiled, and her eyes softened. "I will," she said, "Do a good one, that is. Thank you."

Observations

- Enterprise Architecture is about investing in structural innovations that enhance performance

- Check the extent to which your measures of project performance are about implementation or investment

- There can be a conflict between what the culture values as core capabilities and the actual core capabilities you need

- In the absence of a Board-level Chief Officer for Enterprise Investment, that role must be fulfilled by the CEO

- An Investment Management Office (IMO) is different from a Program Management Office (PMO).

EIGHT

Sam

Sam Hilton is our SVP of Human Resources (HR). At the time of the events I'm telling you about, he had already been with the company for seventeen years. He knew it when it was a much smaller enterprise. Sam has experienced numerous changes in leadership, different corporate strategies and our substantial growth into a global leader. Yet, as much as we know about Sam the Head of HR, we still know relatively little about Sam the man. That's how he likes it, and I respect his choice of boundaries.

I confide in Sam more than I do many people. He is a fantastic listener, completely trustworthy, and careful with his advice. In private, he's always called me Mikey, which is what my parents called me as a boy. Apart from my wife, Laura, he's the only other person who knows that. The next time I move to a new company, I will do everything I can to take Sam along with me.

The day after my meeting with Becky, I flew to Shanghai. China is a strategically important market for us, and the Chinese approach to enterprise is, in some respects, quite different from - for example - the USA and Europe. It's important for me to be there from time-to-time. Sam also happened to be in Shanghai, so I suggested we find some time for the conversation I wanted. We both stayed in the Jin Mao Tower. If you're interested in architecture, check it out. It was designed by an American architect who works for a firm in Chicago. The building's proportions are based upon the number eight, which is associated with prosperity in Chinese culture. The same architect designed the Burj Khalifa in Dubai.

My room was on the 80th floor, with floor-to-ceiling windows facing the Huangpu River and beyond it, the Bund.

I met Sam in the hotel bar, high up on the 87th floor. He asked how I was, which from him, is never just the polite question it might seem to be.

"Upset about the disaster in South Africa. Disoriented by some conversations I'm having about investing in change."

"Our people in South Africa handled things as best as they could."

"I know, and I'm proud of them for that."

"Did you tell them?"

"Yes. But, I probably sounded to them like the big boss from abroad, simply saying the right things."

"Maybe. Were you?"

"No."

Sam paused and looked at the view out of the window, before asking me to tell him about my disorientation. I told him the story so far, from the bathtub all the way to the meeting with Becky. When I finished, Sam said he liked the name Enterprise Investment, then chose to ask me about a detail from deep in the middle of everything I'd said, which is often what he does.

"Have you concluded, yet, why you were niggled by Howard's comment about 'only trying to help'?"

I told him I thought I'd forgotten all about it. I hadn't even realized I'd mentioned it to him, until he pointed it out.

He asked, with obvious care, "Would you like me to suggest a reason why?"

"Yes."

"What do you know of Eric Berne's classic work on human behavior?"

"Are you talking about Transactional Analysis?"

"Specifically, Games People Play."

"Yes. I know that book."

"That's why I think Howard's comment niggled you. It may not be the reason he said it, but in Berne's work, there's a game with a very similar name."

"There is. That's true. I'm Only Trying To Help You."

Sam continued, "Yes, that's the one. So, let's theorize for a moment. Assume Howard's comment, and the context in which he spoke it, was a fleeting glimpse of our culture around creating value from change."

"You mean, people genuinely trying to help others in ways that don't seem to work, and when it's suggested it might be their fault, say something along the lines of 'I was only trying to help'."

"Yes."

"Interesting," I said. "That wouldn't be the only game in play, either. And, while we're theorizing about culture, and on a related note, how about Karpman's Drama Triangle?"

"Victim, Persecutor, Rescuer?"

"Indeed," I confirmed.

"In which case, Howard might have been speaking as a genuine supporter of Lucy's efforts — and therefore from outside the triangle — or from the position of Rescuer."

"Of course, in his own mind he might have been doing the former, not noticing Lucy positioning him as the latter. Then, once I started probing Lucy about her Business Case, she positioned me as a Persecutor, and so the drama unfolds."

"Theoretically."

"Of course."

Sam suggested we take a step backwards and consider the relevance of that Howard-Lucy-Michael cameo to our objective for Enterprise Investment. He observed, "There are, undoubtedly, all sorts of games and dramas playing out in our culture. By overlaying such things as organizational structures and governance processes, we encourage behaviors that help us win, and disarm those that don't."

I challenged him gently on that last point, "Disarm, or channel to our advantage."

"I expect you're right. I'm always more of an idealist than you. But then, I don't have to answer to the Investors and Wall Street."

I smiled, and then suggested, "It seems to me that Enterprise Investment is offering us something of a strategic challenge. We have to drive our culture to create value from change, by channeling the games and dramas that are bound to take place."

Sam smiled in return. "Yes. It seems that we do."

"Hmm. I was thinking of making Simon our Chief Officer for Enterprise Investment, with Ivan as the SVP for Enterprise Architecture and someone new as the SVP for Investing in Change. What's your view on that?"

"Simon would need a lot of support from you and me. And, I suggest, from Wendy. Communications would be vital."

"You're right."

"And," Sam asked, "what about Howard?"

"We'll need to keep an eye on how he reacts."

"OK," Sam said, meaning that he was in overall agreement with the tactics we'd discussed.

Although Sam had suggested that Wendy be included, he and she usually took very different positions on how best to win. But, I took his suggestion as genuine, while noting that none of us are entirely immune to the games and dramas that he and I had briefly discussed.

Then I told Sam about Becky, and asked what it would take to offer her the role of SVP of Investing in Change. "Leave that to me," he said. "I'll tell you what I need from you, if and when I need it."

Finally, I talked to him about having a Chief Officer for Sourcing. He asked me how that differed from Procurement. "That's only one aspect," I explained. "Sourcing is about having everything our enterprise needs to create the value we want, day-in and day-out, whenever and wherever it's needed, and as efficiently as possible. And the more 'cloud-like' we become, through outsourcing, partnerships, and so on, the better at sourcing we have to be."

"When you said 'everything', are you just talking about products and services?"

"And people. I should have said everyone and everything."

"And people," Sam repeated, as he absorbed the potential implications for HR. "If you chose to go ahead with this idea, do you have someone in mind for the role?"

"Lucy."

"Oh."

Sam looked out of the window again. I doubted he was looking at Shanghai. After a short pause I said. "Lucy and her team are doing sourcing already, but only for a limited scope, which is IT."

"But, so am I, for HR."

"Here's the difference. If the IT fails, Lucy is accountable."

I left Sam to reflect on my reply to his challenge. I thought it likely he was struggling with the idea that HR could end up reporting to IT, yet realizing that wasn't the model I was considering.

I asked Sam where he was heading after China.

"Rio."

"Wendy's at home in Melbourne right now, so I'll be heading there next."

"See you back in New York City."

"Enjoy Rio."

"Thanks, Mikey."

Observations

- Different cultures have different approaches to enterprise

- Investment cultures and behaviors are subject to the same 'games' and 'dramas' as anything else

- We overlay organizational structures and governance processes on a culture to encourage behaviors that help us win, and to disarm (or channel to our strategy's advantage) those that don't

- Procurement is only one aspect of Sourcing

- Sourcing includes people, as well as products and services.

NINE

Wendy

Wendy Martin is our flamboyant Chief Officer of Corporate Communications, an Australian, and a great storyteller. She often introduces herself with "My name is Wendy, darling," in an accent that is an unusual and charming mix of East-Coast America and South-East Australia. Only a handful of people realize she is making a reference to the character in Peter Pan, whom her parents named her after. For the same reason, she has a grown-up daughter called Jane, and two teenage sons called James and Matthew. That's our Wendy. Just about everything she says has a story lurking behind it, which you'll probably only discover if it occurs to you to ask.

Partly because of her role, but also because she's Wendy, she often finds an unexpected angle on subjects and events. For example, the objective that Ivan and I agreed on for Enterprise Investment refers to 'performance'. For many people, performance equals our business results, but Wendy champions its theatrical meaning. In our Experiences-Oriented Architecture, Wendy's angle on performance is a vital one to remember.

One of her favorite sayings is "It's our performance that delivers our performance". It's a saying that some people love and others hate, which means at least they're likely to remember it. Because my own background is in Brand and Marketing, I think I have more empathy than many with Wendy's view of performance and how it applies, in practice, to an enterprise, its architecture, and its day-to-day operations.

After meeting Sam in Shanghai, I continued on to Melbourne, Wendy's home. Every time I fly across Australia I am struck by its sheer emptiness. It is over three-quarters of the size of the USA, but its population is less than eight percent. The United Kingdom, for example, is home to nearly three times as many people. Yet, Australia has a very strong identity around the world, and is up there with the best, both economically and in sport, among other things. As I looked out the plane window with nothing to see but endless red desert, I reflected once again on how in the USA, China, Australia, the UK, and everywhere else, there are enterprising people, each with their own particular culture and ways of succeeding.

Wendy has a beautiful art deco house in the Kew area of Melbourne. It's much more pleasant to stay there than in a hotel, and she loves having house guests. She and her husband George are renowned for their parties, with live bands and dancing into the early hours. That day, he and their children were out, so the house was quiet for the two of us to talk.

We sat in Wendy's main living room. I showed her the Investment Culture Diagnosis, and talked about the conversations I'd been having.

"I think you're last," I told her. "After this, I'm going to decide what - if anything - to do. What do you think?"

"What a wonderful challenge," Wendy replied. "What's the word out there?"

"The word?"

"What's the market saying about all of this?"

"That it's an IT problem."

"That's what I hear. But, if I didn't know anything about it I would have thought you were joking."

"Yes," I agreed, "it could be an investment problem, a finance problem, a people problem, a sourcing problem, a communications problem. Or all of those things, and others besides. But not an IT problem."

"Our wonderful challenge, then, is this. People seem to think that the reason we're not achieving the most value we can from our investments in change has something to do with IT. We know that it isn't. It's about our culture and structure, choices, games, and dramas. Ultimately, it's about people, and how they channel their spirits of innovation and enterprise. So, let's say you decide to have a corporate strategy, and Chief Officer, for Enterprise Investment. Communication is obviously going to be core to their success."

"Yes," I agreed.

Wendy was on a roll, already. "Behaviors are the key. That starts with us. As a Board, we have to accept that we are part of the culture and structure that needs to change. So, I think you're right to look at the Board's structure. But, at the same time, I expect there are some careful adjustments in behavior that we would need the Board to make, that would be amplified by the culture and, if our strategy is good enough, would result in us achieving the objective."

She continued, "When I listened to your story, I thought of a picture. A value chain, but different from the Porter Value Chain we all know. One for Enterprise Investment. Wait, while I find some paper." Wendy left the room and came back with a pad of paper and a pen. She drew the picture below:

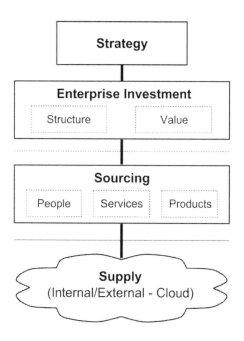

Enterprise Investment - Core Value Chain

Strategy

Enterprise Investment
Structure   Value

Sourcing
People   Services   Products

Supply
(Internal/External - Cloud)

Wendy explained, "All that work that Simon's done on Enterprise Architecture has given us the 'structure' half of Enterprise Investment. Your bathtub moment was a reflection of how much better we need to get at the 'value' half. The conversations you've had with Lucy, Ivan, and Sam about Sourcing are also an essential part of the chain."

I said, "I like your picture."

"Good. I'll make some coffee, then well get back to communications and behaviors."

Wendy disappeared to make us both some coffee. When she came back, I asked her, "If you were me, what would you do?"

"I'd do something, rather than nothing. I think we are currently diluting our success in ways that we can deal with. And, I'm sure we have a duty to act on what you've found - a duty to our employees, customers, and investors."

"I'm concerned about the risk."

"What, of making things worse?"

"That, and having to admit we have a management problem that has previous gone unreported, unnoticed, and unresolved."

"Yes, you're right to be concerned. I believe there are lots of enterprises with exactly the same problem, but that doesn't help. Let's backtrack. Tell me again. How did you notice it in the first place?"

"Lucy's Business Case for her IT transformation program. The bathtub, remember?"

"And the word out there is that this is an IT problem?"

"That's what we said earlier."

Wendy stood up, walked over to her fireplace, turned to face me, and said, "I feel a strategy emerging."

Sensing what she was doing, I stood up, too, and joined her at the fireplace, with us both looking out into the room.

I expected Wendy to break into a dramatic quote, or make up something that sounded like one. Instead she said, "Exactly. Let's sit down and drink our coffee."

Wendy, had, of course used a very simple example of communicating with behavior, rather than words. It was time to dig myself out of the detail, step away, turn around, look back, and think strategically.

As we drank our coffee, she said that achieving the objective that I had originally discussed with Ivan depended upon a change in behavior by our corporate and local executives. That would, in turn, change the way our culture behaved towards investing in change.

"How big a change in executive behavior?" I asked her.

"That would vary by executive. Some might find it a small change, others an insurmountable one."

"Based on how much they feel the subject is important to them and how much value they put on the way we currently behave - whatever their reasons."

"Yes," Wendy agreed.

"To put it another way, some will be the agents of stability, while others, the agents of change."

"And some, like you and me, the agents of strategy, investment, value, and structure. That picture you drew with Ivan is a particularly valuable one. I think it might help people if we show it to them."

"Yes. I agree."

I could see Wendy moving into storytelling mode. She stood up again and said, randomly walking around, "OK, Michael. Imagine you are giving a conference speech in a few years' time. The audience are your peers, some analysts, and some journalists. You tell them our story. At the end, there is a short silence and then warm applause. Some questions come from the floor, some of which are genuine, some designed to probe how much gloss you have put on. Whatever the motive behind the questions, they all discover more depths to our story. Those who were genuinely seeking more clarity like your answers. Any who thought they were going to catch you out feel slightly aggrieved. When the event ends, at least half the CEOs there go away planning to make some changes, to emulate what we've achieved here. Some others will simply be happy, because you've re-affirmed what they've already done. The remainder, however many that is, will mentally file all of this in 'too risky', 'not required', or both."

I sat quietly.

Wendy got to the punch-line. "Now, if that was someone else speaking and you were in the audience, which of those three groups would you be in when the event ended?"

When she's operating in this mode, I know that Wendy's story, and the question at the end, contain twists and complexities that are worth exploring before giving an answer. I stood up slowly, walked over to her living room window, and looked out at her back yard. She has a veranda across the rear of her house, and I asked if I could go and stand on it for a while.

"Sure," she said. "I'll make some more coffee. See if you can spot some parakeets."

One of the reasons I like to visit Wendy at home is that, in Melbourne, you're a long way from almost everywhere. There's space to think, and a sense that you're almost looking back at the rest of the world, seeing it from a distance. Of all the places I could find myself considering the implications of her story and question, the veranda overlooking her garden was probably the best.

"All three," I told her, as she came out with our coffee. I continued with an explanation, "When I got out of the bath after reading Lucy's Business Case, deep down I wanted to make some changes. I had no doubt that we're doing something wrong, that it's harming our performance, and we can make things better. But, there are some good things we are already doing that we need to protect and encourage, not destroy. At the moment, unless you know otherwise, we are not being required to do anything along these lines by either our investors or regulators. And culture change is especially risky. Riskier, for example, than changing our structure."

"I understand," said Wendy. "So, go back to my scenario. Imagine we are now writing your speech, you and me. Remember, there are analysts and journalists in the room, as well as other CEOs. Before you get to talk about the changes we made and how they enhanced our performance, why did we make them?"

"I'd go back to basics. SWOT. Building on our strengths, removing some weaknesses, taking opportunities, and pre-empting threats."

"Could you do it without the Weaknesses?"

"I get your drift. I think we can infer the Weaknesses, without publicly shooting ourselves in the foot."

"Good. But what is your SWOT talking about?"

"Enterprise Investment. Delivering the structure and value we need, as efficiently as we can."

"OK. I can see the Strengths, and I can infer the Weaknesses. If I'm another CEO, I'll know we have some of those Weaknesses, too. But what about the Opportunities and the Threats? Unless you want to suggest that we've been underperforming, they need to be external, real, and worth the risks that come with the change you describe."

"Sure."

Wendy looked out at her estate, then back at me, and said, "Let's go back inside. I want you to show me again, the thing you did with that guy, Ian Taylor. What was it called?"

"Investment Culture Diagnosis."

"That's it. Let's have another look."

I showed Wendy the completed Diagnosis:

Investment Culture Diagnosis

Dimension	Prevailing Culture			
Value Creation	Considered Always	Considered Last	Avoided	Considered First
Innovation Focus	None	Market	Technical	Internal
Investment Portfolio	Inventory	Bottom-Up	Non-Existent	Top-Down
Targeting	Outcomes	Activities	Outputs	None
Exploiting Assets & Services	Central	Missing	Peripheral	Intended
Investment Strategy	Random	Strategic Goals	Operational Goals	Something Else
Sponsorship	Accountable	Nominal	Absent	Responsible
Project Management	Delivering Change	Time/Cost/Quality	ROI Hypothesis	Delivering Value
Impact on Operating Costs	Important	Ignored	Interesting	Critical
Behavior Towards Projects	Controlling	Influencing	Undermining	Not Interested

I could see her eyes move around it as she assimilated the connections in what she saw. She said, "Given what we talked about earlier, I think we have our answer right here. The truth of the matter is that we're not going to make all of this public. But, there are some rows that form the Strengths of your story, and others that we legitimately need to change in light of external Opportunities and Threats. I need to apologize to Ian in his absence; I didn't notice the underlying narrative of his one-pager when you first showed it to me. My bad, as you Americans say!"

"You know I hate apologies. No apologies, no regrets, remember. What do you see?"

"Ends and means. Causes and effects."

"What about the SWOT?"

"OK. Let's use the Investment Culture Diagnosis to construct a future back-story."

"I've got a better idea," I countered, "let's get some of our people to do it for us."

"You're right. That is a better idea. Knowing how fast your mind works, you may as well tell me what you're thinking."

"If Simon's going to end up leading this strategy, he and his new team need to propose it to us. That's the way it always has to work. We're not going to rescue him by coming up with the strategy ourselves. The day anyone else starts dictating your strategy to you, you've lost."

"So you, me, and the other executives will be a sounding-board for Simon and his team?"

"More than that," I said, "we have to decide whether we want to invest ourselves in the strategy Simon proposes. For that, there will need to be a quid-pro-quo for each of us, undoubtedly different in each case."

"Ha! That sounds like the TV show we call Dragons' Den in Australia, and is called Shark Tank in the USA. The one where people who have a business idea propose it to a number of investors, who then subject the proposer to some probing questions before declaring whether they're in or out."

"Almost exactly like that," I replied, "Except in the TV show, the investors act as individuals. In our case, we all represent the same investor."

"Now there's a comment about investment culture!" Wendy exclaimed. "That show started in Japan, and is called Money Tigers there. In some other countries they are lions. Ha! Sharks, Dragons, Tigers, Lions. Animal spirits!"

I smiled at her reference to Enterprise and Economics, and then said, "At this stage, I am limiting the sharks to an inner-circle. Sam, Howard, you, and me. People, money, communications, and corporate strategy. I'll instruct Simon the day after tomorrow, when I'm back in New York."

"What about Lucy, to represent technology? I notice you've included her in your walkabout, but not in the sharks."

"She has a decision to make about where she wants to play in future. Technology or Sourcing. When she's made up her mind, I'll decide."

"I understand. By the way, do I have to be a shark? I'd rather be a dragon," Wendy half-joked.

"Sure. Some people see you as one anyway. It will add to the diversity."

Observations

- Problems with investing in change are frequently treated as an 'IT problem'

- The value chain for Enterprise Investment is different from Porter's

- In any strategy dealing with a management problem that's previously gone unresolved, communications are especially sensitive

- Story-telling and scenarios are valuable techniques in formulating tactics and communications

- In any strategy, some people find the required behavioral changes relatively easy, while others find them insurmountable

- Make sure you know, protect, and encourage your culture's existing strengths, while fixing any weaknesses.

TEN

Strategy

Waiting in the lounge at Melbourne Airport, I got a call from Sam to say that Becky should be joining us within the following six weeks. He had conducted an HR interview with her by phone, and asked her to negotiate the earliest release possible with Ian. Knowing how much she wanted to get home, and owing her a favor or two, Ian had said she could leave as soon as she handed-over to her next in line. I thanked Sam for working so quickly.

With an existing SVP of Enterprise Architecture and a potential successor, and an incoming SVP of Investing in Change, it was time to formulate our strategy for Enterprise Investment.

I got Trudy to book an entire half day for Simon and me, as soon as we both had the time. Given my schedule, and his, that was over three weeks after I got back from Australia. The delay wasn't a problem, as we were under no pressure to act, except from ourselves.

I also needed to spend as much time as I could on the aftermath of the accident in South

Africa. As well as causing all those deaths and injuries it had, as you'd expect, it affected our share price on the NYSE. The way we'd responded to it meant that there would probably be few, if any, longer-term losses. But the sooner we knew the cause, the better. Preliminary findings pointed to some changes that had recently been made to the plant to increase its productivity. I demanded to know whether we were looking at poor design, poor sourcing, poor execution, or poor governance. It turned out it might be all four. The design and execution were both subcontracted to other companies, as is often the case, so we needed to look very hard at our own local capabilities in the sourcing and governance of change.

The communications challenge for Wendy was to ensure that we were transparent about the accident and its cause, and took proper accountability for the consequences, while looking after the victims and their families, and protecting our shareholders' investment.

It was a tough reminder of the kind of friction we do need to have in our process for investing in change. Never mind Business Cases and NPVs, is the change properly designed, properly sourced, properly executed, and properly governed? We might deliver all sorts of value by exploiting changes done well, but we can as-sure-as-hell lose it from changes done badly.

When the time came to sit down with Simon, I took us off-site to my club on East 55th Street. I told him I would give him a download and would answer any questions at the end. I spoke, uninterrupted, for two hours, while Simon wrote pages of notes. When I had finished, he asked if we could take a break so he could collect his thoughts and formulate some questions.

"Sure," I said. "If you need to take a proper break, go for a walk. Take a look at the club's art collection."

Simon took my advice and disappeared for half an hour. When he returned, he said, "I've picked out what I think are the top ten themes. I'll tell you what they are, so that you can set me straight."

"OK."

Simon sat down and listed the themes on a sheet of paper, saying them as he did:

1. *Investment versus Finance*

2. *Investing in change, executing change, exploiting change*

3. *Portfolio of Investments, Investment Management Office*

4. *Delivering both value and structure*

5. *Investment culture, games, and dramas*

6. *Shark Tank, Dragons' Den, etc.*

7. *Animal spirits, enterprise, behavioral economics*

8. *Business Cases or Investment Proposals?*

9. *Communicating through behaviors*

10. *Accountabilities*

I told Simon that was a great list to be starting with. He asked me whether I had decided for sure to have a Chief Officer for Enterprise Investment. I guided him to focus on the strategy and see where it led us. "Don't get distracted by thoughts of your own role. You know what's potentially in the frame. With you and Becky, we now have SVPs for EA and IC, and Ivan as your potential replacement. Bring us your best strategy for EI and we'll take it from there."

"I'd like to bring a preliminary version to you sharks within the next two weeks," he said, "and a final one for ratification a week after that."

"Good. Sort the dates out with Trudy, and include Becky and Ivan in both meetings. Oh, and by the way, Wendy is a dragon."

Simon looked at me with a question on his face.

I just smiled.

"Yes," he said, leaving his unspoken question unanswered, "I'll talk to Trudy."

"You didn't take my bait," I told him, smiling back.

"No, I didn't," he replied, trying not to laugh before he managed to say his punch-line. "I may not share your opinions of Wendy, but I defend your right to have them."

I laughed, and then said, "Make it a great strategy."

Two weeks later, I was in the Boardroom with fellow sharks Howard and Sam, and Wendy the dragon, waiting for Simon, Ivan, and Becky. We had asked Trudy to hold them outside for a few moments because Sam had some news on the South African accident. He had already told me privately, and I wanted him to share it with Howard and Wendy as soon as possible.

"We think we've found the underlying cause of what happened," Sam said. "The reason I'm telling you now is because it's about investment and sourcing, people and culture. It may be a local problem, or more widespread. That's what we are going to find out next. Three years ago, our South African colleagues outsourced some maintenance capabilities. It's a good contract, which is saving us significant amounts of operating cost - just as the original Business Case said it would. I tracked it down and checked it." Sam looked at Howard carefully, as he continued, "Until the accident, it was looking like a very healthy return on our investment in the change." I could see Howard struggling to keep his hands still. Then Sam turned to Wendy. "You'll remember, Wendy, that it figured quite prominently in their communications strategy." Wendy nodded. "But, here's the problem. The people who had previously managed those capabilities in-house have been covertly competing with the external supplier. They haven't been able to tear themselves away from the idea that they still 'provided' those capabilities to the rest of the company, even though it should have been obvious to them that they were now accountable for sourcing the capabilities, not providing them."

"How did that lead to the accident?" I asked.

"Well, there was a certain amount of game-playing going on between our people and the supplier. Most of it was the usual kind, and mostly harmless. But, in the case of the accident, our people signed-off on a change without checking it properly. I think they believed the supplier would be to blame if the change didn't quite work right. It was only a small change."

Sam left that last observation hanging in the air. The scale of any change is not, of course, a reliable indicator of the risk involved.

"Any questions?" Sam asked.

Howard had a question. "I can see this all relates to the strategy discussion we're about to have, but I think it would be helpful if you could summarize why."

"OK," Sam replied, "So here's a change we've invested in, which has achieved the benefits that its Business Case promised. Operationally and technically, the project was implemented really well. We need to give our South African colleagues credit for that. A lot of similar projects struggle where they have succeeded. But, it ultimately depended on structural and behavioral changes that now, with the benefit of hindsight, we can see haven't worked. Our people have been left, possibly even encouraged, to think that they were still providing capabilities long after that stopped being true, and they should be sourcing them instead. They have been channeling time and energy into covertly competing with the actual provider. That's constrained them, and us, from making the very most of the change, and ultimately - in this case - led to the loss of twenty-six lives and over one hundred injured people. In the strategy that Simon's just about to come in and tell us about, we need to make sure it's focused on the structural and behavioral aspects of change, not just the operational and technical aspects. Also, the sad events in South Africa have exposed another change we need to invest in there, probably in some of our other businesses, and possibly everywhere. As our operating model has progressively become more 'virtual', or cloud-like, through outsourcing and the like, we haven't sufficiently built-up our sourcing capabilities. Now we have to."

"Thank you," Howard said.

"Wendy, any questions?" I asked, preparing to move on to the main reason we were together.

"Not now," she said.

"In which case," I concluded, "let's get them in."

I stood up and walked over to the Boardroom door, opened it, smiled, and said, "We're ready. All yours."

Simon took the door from me and held it open for Becky and Ivan. He came into the Boardroom last, quietly shutting the door behind him. When I had sat back down, he asked, "Do you mind if we sit down too?"

Before I could answer, Howard said, "Are you going to present sitting down?"

"No," Simon said, "we haven't brought a presentation with us. We would, however, like to talk this through with you." As he spoke he took a few sheets of paper out of a plastic folder and handed us all one each.

"Fine with me," I said. I looked at the other executives, and they all nodded.

"Thank you," Simon started, but before he could continue, Sam asked, "Is this your proposed strategy?", holding up the one sheet of paper.

"No," said Becky, looking at Ivan and Simon, then at Sam, and then me, as she said, "We are."

While keeping eye contact with Becky, I concentrated on sensing the reactions from Wendy, Sam, and Howard. In fact, they all turned to look at me.

I said, "You'd better sit down. We're all ears."

Simon, Ivan, and Becky sat down at the Boardroom table, on the chairs nearest to the rest of us. Simon continued, "I'm going to briefly tell you how we formulated our proposed strategy. Then, we'll talk you through the written summary in front of you. After that, we will take your questions. After this meeting, we will finalize the strategy and come back to you for final ratification."

I thought Simon had used an interesting choice of words. As close as he probably dared to an 'assumptive close'. Nobody, including me, said anything in response to his opening, so he continued.

"First, we explored and agreed on the 'promise' of our strategy - that is, the outcome it will be focused on achieving, every minute of every day..."

"Simon," I interrupted. "Let's cut to the promise and how you would lead us to achieve it. If the way you formulated the strategy proves to be relevant, we can cover it in our questions."

"Of course," Simon replied. "The strategy's promise is based on the objective that Michael and Ivan discussed, which we have refined and shortened. This is it: our investments in change will collectively deliver our goals for both value and structure, as efficiently as possible." He stopped talking, knowing how much was woven into that one sentence.

Sam, Howard, Wendy, and I were all looking at the sheet of paper in front of us. Deliberately or not, the way that Simon had so far conducted proceedings had led us to take a deep interest in the few words about the strategy he had spoken, and those that he and his team had written. This is what we were reading:

Our Strategy for Enterprise Investment (Draft)

Promise

Our investments in change will collectively deliver our goals for both value and structure as efficiently as possible

Key Principles

A. We invest in change only to produce outcomes we cannot get from existing investments
B. Our goals for investing in change evolve over time
C. 'Value' is a diverse portfolio of measures that come from our strategies and business plans
D. The structure our investments deliver both enables and constrains our future development
E. Investment is about scenarios and probabilities, not certainties

Core Tactics

1. Measure and grow the company's performance in efficiently delivering our goals for investing in change
2. Replace Business Cases with Investment Proposals
3. Prioritize investments based on their impact on value and structure, versus their costs to P&L
4. Appoint full-time Investment Project Managers
5. Inspire people to deliver as much value as they can from every investment that we make

I looked around at my executive colleagues to see who would like to ask a question. Wendy nodded, and said to Simon, "Why five? Five Key Principles, five Core Tactics."

Simon replied without hesitation, "A couple of reasons. First, we want to make this as easy to remember as we can. So we chose to keep the Principles and Tactics to the number of fingers on each hand." As he spoke that last sentence, he held up both his hands, fingers splayed, to emphasize the point. "Second," he continued, "we want to concentrate on the most significant Principles and Tactics. The ones that we think will drive everything else."

"Thank you," said Wendy, "I'm not sure yet whether these are the best Principles and Tactics, but I agree with your approach."

"Howard?" I prompted.

"Yes."

"Questions?"

"Yes. Core Tactic number three. The one about P&L. Please talk it through and tell me why you've not mentioned capital investment anywhere."

Simon turned to Becky. She said, "Day-to-day operations are the source of our value. It's a mistake to think that change, in itself, delivers value. Changing our operations results in them delivering more value, the same value, or less than they would have done anyway. They will also be structured better, the same, or worse. So, we need to concentrate on costs to P&L, rather than capital. Those costs include the depreciation that capex causes."

Becky looked at Howard, to see how he was reacting. He said nothing, and his hands were still. He wasn't giving anything away. She continued, "We also invest time and money in changes while we're designing and implementing them. We can capitalize that investment sometimes, if we choose to, but it's the same time and money we could invest in operations. There's a zero-sum game for us to manage in there somewhere, between operations and change. Then, after we have made a change, we can expect there to be some kind of impact on our operating costs. Those costs may be higher or lower, or distributed differently."

Becky looked at Howard again. Still no visible reaction. "So," she summarized, "as investors, we're focused on the collective impact that changes have on the value our operations produce, on how those operations are structured, and on our costs to P&L."

At last Howard responded. "I'll need to think about that," he said. I had a feeling he wasn't alone.

I turned to Sam next. He looked at Simon and asked, "How do you plan to achieve tactic five, the one about inspiring people? To me, that's the most important one of all, and unlike the other four tactics, isn't worded as a tangible action."

"Yes, Sam, I know," replied Simon, with no hint of defensiveness or doubt. "Ivan, Becky, and I talked about that one a lot. We believe that people are currently being stifled from doing the very thing we would like them to do."

"Which is?" Sam asked.

"As the tactic says, to deliver as much value as they can from every investment that we make."

"Why do you think we are stifling them?"

"I can tell you how we are stifling them, better than why."

Sam didn't react verbally to Simon's answer, but he turned his head slightly, and looked at Simon out of the corner of his eye.

Simon continued, "There are four ways we stifle people. One, by expecting them to think of a change and then 'prove' its value with a Business

Case. Two, by not exiting investments that looked good when they started but have a declining probability of success. Three, by defining success as achieving the Business Case benefits, rather than delivering as much value as possible. Four, by constraining people in what we let them do with a change once we've made it. The result is we are getting much less value than we could from our investments in change. The whole set-up seems to be focused on the people who want to make changes, rather than the people who create value."

At this point, Howard intervened with what he believed was a 'gotcha', which suggested to me he was feeling challenged by Becky's answer to his earlier question. "I thought Becky said it was a mistake to talk about change delivering value."

Becky made to talk, but Simon lifted a finger to indicate he would answer. Good for him. "It's certainly a mistake to think that change, in itself, delivers value. When we talk about getting as much value as we can from our investments in change, then yes, it's from the operations that we've changed."

Simon looked squarely at Howard, who was probably thinking that his 'gotcha' had backfired and said no more. Howard needed to choose his questions more carefully.

Turning back to Sam, Simon said, "On reflection, perhaps we should talk about 'unleashing' people's enterprise, rather than 'inspiring' them."

Ivan spoke, making his first contribution to the discussion. "Unleashing people's enterprise."

I turned to face Ivan. "Yes!" I said, deliberately up-tempo. "That's what this strategy is all about. Unleashing people's enterprise to create value from change. Now we're talking. I was concerned it was all getting a bit technical. This is more like the conversation we need to have."

Ivan spoke again, "The people we are mainly talking about are our company's customers and employees, right?"

Simon replied, "Right."

Ivan continued, "That means most of the unleashing needs to be done by our local businesses, whose customers and employees they are."

Everyone was looking at Ivan, as he developed his theme. "In which case, it's going to be the executives in our business units that need to do the unleashing."

I sensed Wendy smiling. That was an echo of what she'd told me in Melbourne.

Ivan carried on. "We can work with them on the structure, tools, techniques, and so on, but they have to drive the strategy's success."

Simon looked at me and said, "The next global conference for our local CEOs and MDs is in six weeks' time. I think we should launch the strategy then."

"Hold on," I said. "Slow down. We haven't told you if we want to invest in it yet. Let's park that thought about the leadership conference and get back to the process. At the end of this meeting, each of us will need to tell you whether we're in or out. As far as I am concerned, to go ahead with the strategy, we all need to be in. Today, if we give you the green light, it will only be to come back in a week for a final decision." Catching Howard's eye, I added, "There are some risks in all of this that we have yet to consider. They could easily outweigh the benefits, if we're not careful."

I left a few moments of silence, and then said, "I think we should say the extent to which we're currently in, or out. That will tell us how much more time it's worth investing in this today."

Wendy asked, "Shall I go first?"

"Sure."

Addressing Simon, she said, "I'm in, as far as reviewing the final version of this strategy. Next time we see you, I'd encourage you to come prepared to talk more about the dynamics, and less about the technicalities."

"Thank you," Simon, replied.

Howard was the next to declare his position. "You'll need to reassure me that this is not going to descend into a free-for-all. What we have at the moment may not be perfect, but it does make sure we apply some tried-and tested controls. For now, I'm in."

"Sam?" I said.

He was motionless, looking at the Boardroom table. "I'm thinking about behaviors," he said, then looked up at Simon. "We could do everything you've written down and get exactly nowhere. Changing structures, documents, and processes are unlikely to give us the answer, unless we also change culture and behaviors. Next time, can you come prepared to talk about changing people's behaviors? Yes?"

"Yes," Simon agreed.

"Then I'm in."

That left just me.

"Simon, Ivan, Becky," I said, "I'm in. Good work. We'll see you in a week's time for a final decision. This is not a done deal. I've written down the conditions we've all placed on still being in at this stage. Make sure you come back and talk to us about risks, dynamics, controls, and behaviors. OK?"

"OK," they all said together, tidied up their papers, stood up, and left the room.

With just me, Howard, Wendy, and Sam in the room, I said that I thought the global leaders conference would be the best opportunity to announce the strategy if we chose to go ahead. Wendy, whose people were organizing the conference, agreed. The agenda had already been published, so we would have to replace something, or extend one of the days. I told her I just wanted to check it would be feasible, if that's what we chose to do. No need to change anything yet.

A week later, Simon, Becky, and Ivan joined us in the Boardroom again. Simon distributed a revised one-page account of their proposed strategy. Again, it had a five-and-five list of Principles and Tactics, and a shorter Promise. In this one, it was clear they had considered more carefully the roles and values of the people - the sharks and the dragon - who would be deciding whether, or not, to invest:

Our Strategy for Enterprise Investment (Draft 2)

Promise

Our investments in change efficiently deliver our goals for both value and structure

Key Principles

A. We invest in change only to produce outcomes we cannot get from existing investments
B. Our goals for investing in change include both value and structure, and evolve over time
C. 'Value' is a diverse portfolio of measures that come from our strategies and business plans
D. The structure our investments deliver both enables and constrains our future development
E. Investment is about scenarios and probabilities, not certainties

Core Tactics

1. In our business planning, agree on goals and provisions for investing in change
2. Govern investments as a portfolio of outcomes, achieved as efficiently as possible
3. Select investments for their impact on value and structure, versus their costs to P&L
4. Manage projects based on latest probabilities of success, and invoke exit strategies
5. Reward people for delivering as much value as they can from the investments that we make

Simon talked us through the changes they had made. "Based on our discussion last week, about unleashing people's enterprise, we have focused more on dynamics, controls, risks, and behaviors, and less on specific methods or techniques."

"Good," I commented.

Simon continued, "I'll point out the main changes we've made, then we'll take your questions." He looked around for agreement. Nobody said anything, so he carried on, "You'll see we have shortened the Promise and made it the present tense, rather than a statement about the future. I expect few people, if any, would think we are currently achieving it, yet most would agree that we should be. That's more of a call to action than promising to achieve it sometime in the future." Simon paused, then talked about the Principles. "The Principles are almost exactly the same as before, except in the second one, where we have reinforced the focus on both value and structure." Another pause. Then, "We have radically restated the Tactics, making them much more about dynamics and controls, and removing references to specific roles and techniques. Our strategy is now about providing effective direction, boundaries, encouragement, and rewards for people to use their own enterprise to deliver the best possible results."

This time, I decided to ask the first question. "Can you relate this to the Investment Culture Diagnosis that Ian Taylor got me to do? For example, if the strategy succeeds, and we did another diagnosis, what would be different? Also, what does that tell us about the strategy's own probability of success?"

Becky handed Simon some more sheets of paper. Simon carried on talking while he handed us two sheets each. "Here is that current diagnosis and what we think it would look like if the strategy succeeded." It was good to see that they had prepared for the question.

Investment Culture Diagnosis (Current)

Dimension	Prevailing Culture			
Value Creation	Considered Always	Considered Last	Avoided	Considered First
Innovation Focus	None	Market	Technical	Internal
Investment Portfolio	Inventory	Bottom-Up	Non-Existent	Top-Down
Targeting	Outcomes	Activities	Outputs	None
Exploiting Assets & Services	Central	Missing	Peripheral	Intended
Investment Strategy	Random	Strategic Goals	Operational Goals	Something Else
Sponsorship	Accountable	Nominal	Absent	Responsible
Project Management	Delivering Change	Time/Cost/Quality	ROI Hypothesis	Delivering Value
Impact on Operating Costs	Important	Ignored	Interesting	Critical
Behavior Towards Projects	Controlling	Influencing	Undermining	Not Interested

Investment Culture Diagnosis (Strategy)

Dimension	Prevailing Culture			
Value Creation	Considered Always	Considered Last	Avoided	Considered First
Innovation Focus	None	Market	Technical	Internal
Investment Portfolio	Inventory	Bottom-Up	Non-Existent	Top-Down
Targeting	Outcomes	Activities	Outputs	None
Exploiting Assets & Services	Central	Missing	Peripheral	Intended
Investment Strategy	Random	Strategic Goals	Operational Goals	Something Else
Sponsorship	Accountable	Nominal	Absent	Responsible
Project Management	Delivering Change	Time/Cost/Quality	ROI Hypothesis	Delivering Value
Impact on Operating Costs	Important	Ignored	Interesting	Critical
Behavior Towards Projects	Controlling	Influencing	Undermining	Not Interested

Simon looked at Becky and invited her to speak. "In the second version of the diagnosis, we've highlighted the rows that would change, which are all but one of them," she said. "That shows how different our investment culture is here, from those companies that are truly successful at Investing in Change. We're a long way off. So are lots of other companies, believe me."

Wendy asked, "The one row that you haven't changed, about Innovation, why is that?"

Becky replied, "Our innovation focus can be whatever we choose. It's up to our overall corporate strategy, and each of our business strategies, to decide which focus is best. But, we do need to ensure that our investment culture has the same innovation focus as our strategies. Otherwise we'll not get the kinds of innovation we want."

Then Howard asked, "We've put a lot of effort towards making project sponsors accountable. Here you've shown them only as responsible. Why?"

Becky answered again, "Do you fire, or at least penalize, sponsors whose projects fail? Do you reward the ones whose projects succeed? If so, that would be unusual. We need project managers who are accountable for investment success or failure, supported by responsible sponsors."

Howard conceded, saying, "I understand the distinction you're making. Thank you."

Sam asked, "You've got project managers delivering change, and delivering value. Are they the same ones?"

Simon replied, "No. Those are two different types of project management. The first is targeted on outputs, the second on outcomes. Being great at one doesn't mean you're great at the other. And, there's a conflict of interest involved, which means we shouldn't make one person accountable for both."

"Which is...?"

Becky took over the conversation again. "OK. If you look at a performance report for a project, you should see two 'traffic lights'. One is for the probability of a successful implementation, the other for the probability of a successful investment. It's common for the two traffic lights to be different colors. For example, the implementation could be green, meaning it currently has a high probability of success, yet the investment could be amber, meaning a medium probability. Or even black, meaning a recommended exit. We do get projects that are 'green' for implementation and 'black' for investment, and they help to highlight the conflict of interest."

"I've never heard of the two traffic lights before," Sam said. "All of our projects only have one."

Becky treated Sam's last comment as an observation rather than a question, and didn't offer a reply.

I brought us all back to the big picture. "Between us here, we can all see that we're way adrift from being truly effective at creating value from change. From what I read and hear, Becky, I agree with you that many other companies are in the same situation as we are. However, thanks to the work that Simon has been leading since he joined us, we have become increasingly effective, worldwide, at creating structure from change. In that respect, I believe we are much better than many other companies. These two versions of the Investment Culture Diagnosis seem to paint a gloomy picture of our current capabilities. Where do they reflect our strengths?"

Ivan leaned forward. Simon turned towards him and nodded. Ivan said, "Our strengths at investing in structure are reflected in the statements of prevailing culture that are the same in both versions. Innovation in the market and internally. Targeting of outputs. Project management of delivering change. I also differ from you, Michael, in your original diagnosis. I believe our investment strategy is driven by our strategic goals, as far as they are structural. I think the 'something else' you chose refers to Net Present Value." I confirmed this with a nod, so Ivan continued, "But if we think that a project is a good one to invest in strategically, we make sure it exceeds our NPV threshold."

"You're right, Ivan, my diagnosis for that row was wrong. It should be both. Do any of you disagree with my other answers?" Nobody did.

"So," I said, "I'm going to ask Howard, Wendy, and Sam to say whether they are in, or out. Let's see where we all are, to know whether it's worth carrying on this conversation now that we've gotten this far. This time, I'm going first. There's going to be no point in me asking the others if I'm out. Simon, you need to know that Wendy and I had a conversation over in Australia about positioning and communication. As far as anyone outside this room is concerned, this strategy will be building on our strengths, not addressing any weaknesses. It will also need to be driven by external opportunities and threats, not internal ones. That's our SWOT story. It will be authentic, but carefully crafted. So far, so good?"

"Yes," said Simon.

"Right," I continued, "We are also under no pressure from our shareholders or regulators to fix anything along the lines we've been discussing. However, they do examine our performance in getting IT delivered, and in using it to create value. I expect you can see where I'm taking this."

"I can," said Simon, "I've seen it done before."

"Me too," Becky added.

"And I thought I was being original. Anyway, If we understand each other on all of that, Simon, I'm in. Now, Wendy."

"I'm in," Wendy declared.

"Sam?"

"Provided this is a strategy about dynamics and behaviors, I'm in."

"An important condition. Simon," I said, "do you agree?"

"Yes. Agreed."

I finally turned to our CFO, who I expected would be the most cautious. "Howard?"

"In," he said.

"Congratulations, team. Good job," I said to Simon, Ivan, and Becky. "Now, last week we started to explore how to communicate this strategy to the people out there who will make it happen, the local CEOs and MDs. To have any realistic chance of success, we have to remember that our own behaviors will be vital. Strategy is, at its heart, a pattern of behavior." I looked around the room, checking that everyone was tuned-in to their own accountability to behave as our strategy demanded. Then I continued, "To publicly start the ball rolling, let's target the global conference in five weeks' time. Wendy, can you and Simon prepare a presentation for me to deliver?"

"Sure," Wendy replied, smiling at Simon.

"Great," I said, "let's have a draft ready by the end of next week."

When the meeting had finished, I asked Simon to stay behind. He changed chairs to sit next to me, on my right.

I turned to him and asked, "What are your thoughts now, on being the Chief Officer accountable for this strategy?"

"I'm in," he replied.

"Excellent," I told him. "Do a good one."

Observations

- In today's increasingly 'cloud-like' organizations, it's vital that people know the difference between sourcing and supply

- The scale of any change is not an indicator of the risk involved

- The way a strategy is executed is more important than how it's formulated

- In expressing a strategy, a five-and-five approach to Principles and Tactics means discovering the most significant ones that drive everything else

- The essential investment equation is value plus structure versus costs to P&L

- There are at least four ways your approach could be stifling people to achieve the very thing you want them to do

- Investment cultures can become focused on the people who want to make changes, rather than the people who deliver value

- Project performance is based on two 'traffic lights' - one for implementation, the other for investment. They often will be different.

ELEVEN

CEOs, MDs

I'm sure those of you who take an interest in such things will know an emergent strategy when you see one. That was the big bet I was making. The alternative would have been to choose a deliberate strategy, to give our culture and people more structure, more pre-determined answers. My tendency is always to go more emergent than deliberate, which means I need to be careful not to overdo it. Some people love the space that I give them. Others need more structure.

The immediate challenge I faced, with the help of Simon and Wendy, was to give our business leaders enough of both space and structure for our strategy to succeed. I wasn't that surprised when the two of them came to see me, concerned that my conference presentation needed to communicate some more of the 'how' for people than we had so far prepared.

"What kind of 'how' would be best, given the audience?" I asked them.

Simon replied, "Something organizational, something operational, and something technical. That should cover all the bases."

"You had some of that in the first draft of the strategy," I observed.

"That's true," replied Wendy.

Simon added, "Yes, we had a tactic about replacing Business Cases with Investment Proposals. That's operational and technical. We also had one about appointing full-time Investment Project Managers, which is organizational and technical."

"Why technical?" I asked.

"Because we will have to spell out the differences between project-managing the investment and project-managing the implementation, and why it's unwise to have the same person doing both."

"True."

Simon continued, "Becky knows all about strategies for Investing in Change, which is the part we know least about. Can we include in your presentation some more of what she will be leading us to do?"

"Yes, do that," I said. "Now we've gotten this far, we can make that part of our strategy more deliberate, using the processes and techniques Becky knows. And, organizationally, I can add something else, the appointment of a corporate

Chief Officer for Enterprise Investment, and a requirement of each business to appoint one. As a consequence, those that currently have CIO or CTO roles will need to decide where they now fit. I may also couple this with another organizational announcement, but I must talk to Lucy first."

Simon and Wendy said they had what they needed for the moment, and thanked me for my time.

I asked Trudy to get Lucy into my office as quickly as possible. Within the hour, my Chief Technology Officer was sitting with me at my meeting table. No flirting, no joking. She could see from my demeanor that we had serious matters to discuss.

I asked Lucy, "Have you been briefed on the cause of the South African accident?"

"Yes."

"A relatively minor piece of technology maintenance, and a sourcing project that wasn't as successful as we all thought."

"Yes."

I was sure Lucy knew where I was leading. I said, "You're my CTO, and sourcing is your department's core capability."

"Yes, I am, and it is. Never mind my title; the technology in question is not currently in my scope."

"No, it isn't. And as your role stands today, I don't think it should be." Lucy let slip a slight look of relief. I continued, "It's time for you answer the question I asked you. We need a global Chief Officer for Sourcing. I'd like it to be you. I think you're already performing the role, but your scope is too narrow."

"I haven't come back to you because I've been of two minds."

"Level with me. What's the issue."

"Fear."

"Of?"

"Being found out. That I'm only the IT girl, really."

"And I'm only the Brand management guy, really."

"I think not."

"Exactly. It's called the 'imposter syndrome'."

We looked hard at each other.

I said, "So, will you do this for me?"

"I will," She replied.

On Friday of that week, as planned, Simon and Wendy came to my office with my draft presentation for the global leadership conference. It was simple and to the point. No glitz, no glamor, just the strategy we wanted people to explore, question, take away, and act upon. I asked them to make a couple of changes, to better suit my style, and to include an announcement of Lucy's appointment as global Chief Officer for Sourcing.

"Of course," I reminded them, "we can't include this in the conference agenda until I've cleared it with the main Board and we have an announcement ready for the markets. I've put it on the agenda for the Board meeting next week."

The Board meeting came and went, and I got their backing for the changes. They liked the positioning, the blend of emergent and deliberate strategy, and the fact that we were going to better harness people's enterprise, and so make our investments more productive. They were concerned about controls, but Howard dealt with that angle to their satisfaction. They could see that we were unleashing people's enterprise through more controls, not less. Wendy and Howard prepared a statement for the markets, and a press release, both to go out on the morning of our conference, at the same time as I announced the Board changes there. In the conference agenda, we simply billed it as the 'CEO's Update'."

Here's the presentation that I gave:

Investing in Change and IT

It's Time to Upgrade
Our Management Model

Michael F. Rodgers
Global CEO

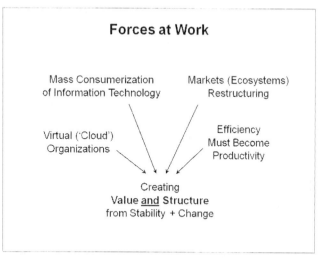

The Bottom Line

- We are great at innovation in the market and internally
- The mass consumerization of the IT market, coupled with the progressive 'virtualization' of enterprises, are major opportunities and threats
- With IT so integral to people's lives and businesses, changes in the structure of the IT market impact every other market
- Customers are using IT to create value for themselves in ways that are radically different from the past
- We need to make sure that they are also creating value for us
- It's time to change the way we think about investing in change and IT
- It's time to change the way we choose, manage, and exploit the investments that we make

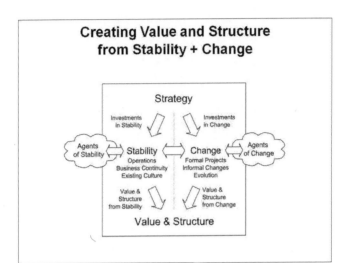

Introducing "Enterprise Investment"

Combining
Enterprise Architecture (Structure)
with
Investing in Change (Value)

underpinned with
exceptional **Sourcing**

and 'virtual' **Supply**

Enterprise Investment – Core Value Chain

Strategy

Enterprise Investment
Structure | Value

Sourcing
People | Services | Products

Supply
(Internal/External - Cloud)

Our Corporate Strategy for Enterprise Investment

What Success Looks Like
Our investments in change efficiently deliver
our goals for both value and structure

The Principles We Need to Apply
✓ We invest in change only to produce outcomes we cannot get from existing investments
✓ Our goals for investing in change include both value and structure, and evolve over time
✓ 'Value' is a diverse portfolio of measures that come from our strategies and business plans
✓ The structure our investments deliver both enables and constrains our future development
✓ Investment is about scenarios and probabilities, not certainties

What We Need to Do
⇨ In our business planning, agree on goals and provisions for investing in change
⇨ Govern investments as a portfolio of outcomes, achieved as efficiently as possible
⇨ Select investments for their impact on value and structure, versus their costs to P&L
⇨ Manage projects based on latest probabilities of success, and invoke exit strategies
⇨ Reward people for delivering as much value as they can from the investments that we make

Organizational Changes

Corporate Chief Officer
for Enterprise Investment
Simon Rathbone

Global SVP – Enterprise Architecture Ivan Bingham

Global SVP – Investing in Change Becky Chekhova

Plus: Enterprise Architects & Investment Project Managers

Corporate Chief Officer
for Sourcing
Lucy Hau

SVPs & Sourcing Managers To be announced

You will need to make similar changes to your local management teams

Process Changes

- Annual Business Plans to include goals and provisions for Enterprise Investment
- Replacing Business Cases with Investment Proposals
  - more about this in a moment
- Executive "Shark Tank" (aka "Dragons' Den") to monitor portfolio goals and performance, and approve/reject Investment Proposals
- Investment Management Office (IMO)
- Routine re-assessment of projects' probabilities of success
  Two traffic lights: implementation; investment
- All projects must include an exit strategy, invoked when probability falls below acceptable level
- NPV required for cash-generating projects only
- Let's not be constrained by the theoretical benefits in the Investment Proposal. Let's always create the best value and structure that we can!
- And let's not forget, it's our customers that create our value

---

Replacing Business Cases
with Investment Proposals

Business Case	Investment Proposal
• Driven by Change	• Driven by Investment Goals
• Purpose: justification	• Purpose: evaluation
• Preferred solution & options	• Gross value* (minimum, optimistic)
• Costs, resources, funding	• Architectural impact
• Benefits	• Costs, resources, funding
• Net value (NPV)	• Options & recommended solution
• Risks & mitigations	• Probability of success (<100%)
	• Risks & mitigations
	• Exit strategy

*Not required for purely structural investments

Not just a different document. A different mindset.

In Summary...

- Opportunities and threats in our markets worldwide
- Time to pull on our strengths at innovation
- Investing in structure and value = Enterprise Investment
- More goal-driven & rigorous in our choice of investments
- Proactively managing probabilities of success
- Exit strategy for every investment
- Structural changes - organization and process
- Unleashing ourselves and our customers to create maximum value from the investments we make

---

It took me about an hour to talk through these eleven slides. Then we opened the session up for questions. Here are the ones that stood out:

Q.   If this is a situation caused by IT, why don't we just change the IT Department's structure and processes?

A.   As I said, IT is now deeply integral to our lives, businesses, and markets. IT is a cause of the opportunities and threats but it isn't, on its own, the answer to them. Simply changing the structure of an IT department won't make the breakthrough we now need.

Q.   With Enterprise Investment and Sourcing, do we still need an IT Department? I noticed that you are not replacing Lucy as CTO.

A.   With Lucy's promotion to Chief Officer for Sourcing, we will no longer have a corporate IT department. We are still designing that part of the structure, but I expect she will have an SVP for each class of goods and services we use, including one for IT. More generally, we believe that our two new Board-level roles make the very best of some core capabilities that IT departments already have. Of course, IT is an integral part of both those roles. You need to decide, locally, what's best for you. If you still see the value in having an IT Department, we'll leave that up to you.

Q.   Are you saying that we're not very good at creating value from change?

A.   For the reasons I said in my presentation, the context has radically changed. We will increasingly struggle with it, if we continue doing it the way that we have in the past.

Q.   How many other companies are doing this?

A.   I don't know, and frankly, I don't care.

Q.   That's the first time I've seen probability of success being explicitly included in Investment Proposals, and being proactively monitored throughout the project. Does that mean we'll only invest in high-probability Proposals?

A.   No. We'll often invest in low-probability projects because of their potential. It's vital that we manage them differently from high-probability projects. It would be a mistake only to invest in high-probability projects, and would probably drive us to, shall we say, be less than prudent in our assessment of probability. (I thought, but didn't say, like only investing in NPV-positive projects.)

Q.   I think our own people need to see this presentation, and explore what it means in practice. Will you be repeating it locally?

A.   No, but you will. Wendy will be sending you the slides, and will be expecting a report-back from you within the next month, when you have made the presentation to your people, with a summary of the questions-and-answers it provoked.

Q.   Are we still going to hold people to their Business Case benefits?

A.   If we absolutely need those benefits, for example for regulatory compliance, then yes. Otherwise we want people to create as much value as they can from the investments that we make, in the context of our strategic and operational objectives. And by people, I mean customers and investors, as well as employees. Oh, and it's Investment Proposal, not Business Case.

The person who asked that final question said "Sorry," in reply to my reminder. A few people around him, who obviously knew me better than he did, turned to look at him and gently shook their heads. The person on his left muttered something in his ear, which I expect was, "Michael hates apologies."

My presentation was deliberately scheduled as the last one before lunch, to give the CEOs and MDs time to think and talk about it before the next session. As people were leaving the conference room, Simon, Becky, Ivan, and Lucy all came over to me.

"Game on," I said. "Let's eat."

Observations

- Choose a careful balance between an emergent and deliberate strategy, depending on what will work best in your enterprise

- In communicating your strategy and tactics, include organizational, operational, and technical considerations

- The 'imposter syndrome' can be a material factor in people accepting and achieving new challenges

- Changing the structure of an IT organization won't - on its own - achieve a breakthrough in the delivery of value from change, even when change is IT-related

- Invest in low-probability projects as well as higher-probability ones, but manage them differently.

TWELVE

Consequences

It's two years, now, since I gave that presentation to our CEOs and MDs. Let me end by telling you what's happened so far, as a result of our strategy. As I promised I would do at the outset, I'll focus on how it has influenced the performance of our company and the motivations of our people. A lot happens in two years, so I'll choose the most significant things to tell you, as I see them.

In my introduction, I told you about the scale of our enterprise. Using the same measures, here's where we are today. We have 59 subsidiaries worldwide. We've acquired three, and disposed of none. We employ 136,000 people, an increase of 11,000. Our total annual revenues are now $104 billion, compared with $89 billion. We've grown our revenues both organically and with those careful acquisitions, in approximately equal amounts. Net profits have increased from $9.5 billion to $17.4 billion, and market capitalization from $64 billion to $75 billion.

But the figure I'm most proud of is how much profit we're now turning across the corporation for each dollar of investment in operating expenses. Overall, it's increased by 68%. In terms of our productivity from investing in both stability and change, we're getting something right, that's for sure.

Note that I called it 'investment in operating expenses'. That's a behavioral change we agreed on at the executive Board after some spirited debate. We've stopped talking about overheads. We decided to treat every cent as an investment, whether that's in our operations today, or our changes for tomorrow and beyond. From my history in Brand, I know that what we call things can make an enormous difference to how people feel about them, and how they behave as a result. That has tangible consequences for the performance of our company. In a productivity-driven strategy, like ours, we want everyone to create as much value as they can from every cent we invest.

Deciding to treat operating costs as investments also had positive consequences for our Enterprise Investment portfolio and its risk-efficiency. The first Principle of our strategy makes it clear why: we invest in change only to produce outcomes we cannot get from existing investments. Tucked away in that Principle is a risk to avoid: wasting investment in changes you don't need to make, when you could achieve your goals with existing operations.

I want to show you how we structure our Enterprise Investment portfolios. Each of our businesses has one, with a Shark Tank of executives to choose, monitor, and govern it. They are all built using the same data model. That makes sure we can aggregate them corporately, and helps businesses spot opportunities to invest in change together, rather than separately.

I've chosen my example from one of our smaller subsidiaries, given the space constraints here, so bear in mind that the numbers are relatively modest:

Enterprise Investment Portfolio

Value Type	Investment Goals		Projects	Value	Project Investment*	P&L Cost Impact	Probability	
	This Year	Next Year					Implementation	Investment
Revenue protection & growth	+$125.0m	+$150.0m	Project A	+$13.5m	$9.2m	+$0.32m	High	Medium
			Project B	+$131.8m	$32.6m	+$3.18m	Medium	Medium
			Project C	+$11.2m	$11.2m	+$4.01m	High	Low
Cost control & reduction	-$75.0m	+/- $0m	Project D	-$26.8m	$2.4m	+$1.88m	Medium	High
			Project E	-$83.7m	$16.4m	+$7.98m	High	High
Productivity	+0.5	+1.0	Project F	+0.31	$8.9m	-$0.70m	Medium	Low
			Project G	+0.63	$10.8m	+$2.85m	Medium	Medium
Brand reputation	+5.0%	To Be Confirmed	Project H	+3.0%	$6.5m	+$1.06m	Low	Low
			Project I	+8.5%	$4.1m	+$5.23m	High	Medium
Customer delight	+0.25	+0.40	Project J	+0.21	$5.6m	+$2.76m	High	High
			Project K	+0.16	$19.5m	+$3.05m	High	High
Operational Safety	Gold	Gold	Project L	Yes	$26.3m	+$5.64m	High	High
Employee satisfaction	+5.0%	+5.0%	Project M	+9.5%	$4.7m	-$0.30m	High	Low
Regulatory Compliance	Yes	Yes	Project N	Yes	$7.9m	+$2.28m	High	Medium
Enterprise **Architecture**	Yes	Yes	Project O	Yes	$31.4m	+$13.28m	High	Medium
Survival	Yes	Yes	Project P	Yes	$0.3m	+$4.10m	High	High
					$197.8m	+$40.66m		

*Project Investment = actual cash + cash equivalent of employees' time

What you're looking at is a snapshot of that business's portfolio on a particular day. Within days, it would look different. It's not a static account of their investments. Each portfolio is alive and changing all the time.

As well as starting new projects and ending existing ones, our Investment Project Managers are routinely updating probabilities and making sure we act quickly on the results. We've also become accustomed to projects moving between value types. As the world changes around them, and we discover the difference between the real project and its original hypothesis, it's not unusual to find it will deliver different value than we first thought. We've given these projects a name, which is itself designed to emphasize our changes in culture and behaviors. We call them 'Blue Pill Projects', a reference both to the film The Matrix, and to the drug Viagra[5]. The Matrix, because the original value of the project has become an illusion. Viagra, because that drug was originally developed for the treatment of different medical conditions from the one for which it proved to be valuable.

Take a look at the portfolio above. If these were your goals, and your projects, what would you choose to do next? In particular, you're not

---

[5] Viagra® is a registered trademark of Pfizer Inc. The drug itself is actually sildenafil citrate. What's in a name, eh?

going to achieve your goals for Customer Delight unless you do something soon.

Notice how we plan for projects to overshoot our goals, to allow for those that deliver less value than we expect, for 'Blue Pill' projects, and for those we decide to exit.

Also, there is no net value, even for projects with financial benefits. It's better to track gross value and costs when comparing the merits and performance of different investments. It also helps to avoid the trap of 'compensating errors' during a project's execution, where updated forecasts of its benefits and costs offset each other - potentially similar net value as before, but no longer achieving your goals.

Something else we have worked on a lot is setting goals for our investments that are both achievable and measurable. As obvious as it may sound, we've found this quite testing.

In setting achievable goals, Enterprise Investment is no different from anything else. The goals can be stretching, BHAGs[6] even, but still be realistic. We have to take our real-world

---

[6] Big, Hairy, Audacious Goals

performance and capabilities into account. As we get better at Enterprise Investment, the more audacious our investment goals are becoming.

Setting measurable goals proved to be harder than setting achievable ones.

For example, it can be hard to know whether a performance improvement has been caused by a particular project, or by a combination of changes, or would have happened anyway. Let's say we target a project to deliver a $30 million increase in revenues. If it's by launching a new product or service, no problem. We can measure that. But, if it's from our existing products and services, any increases in revenues could be caused by all kinds of things. Also, how long after the project's implementation do we need to wait before concluding that it's been a successful investment, or not? The longer we have to leave it, the less we will know whether a performance improvement came from the project or from something else.

Becky, of course, already had the answer. It's to focus each Investment Proposal on the outcome we can confidently use to measure the project's success. But, knowing the answer was relatively easy. The hard part has been changing our behaviors to act on that knowledge, and keeping it that way. It has required yet more transparency, and more prudence.

In practice, it means investing more in leading indicators of performance, and less in trailing indicators. For example, if we don't believe we'll be able to tell if a project's delivered a revenue improvement, then we invest in a related, leading indicator of future revenue - such as Customer Delight, or Brand Reputation - and drive the project using that.

I can't imagine how we could do that, effectively, without Enterprise Architecture. You've got to know the cause-and-effect relationships in your structure. In the example above, if you want to deliver revenue growth, indirectly, by investing in change, you've got to know what leading indicators to invest in, and why that would work. And, notice when it doesn't. There comes a point where increasing customer delight will cause you to get no more revenue than you would have gotten anyway.

Alongside our strategy's impacts on our performance, and our investment choices, it has also had consequences for our culture and motivations.

Our Investment Culture doesn't yet match the target diagnosis that Simon, Ivan and Becky produced for our strategy. I'm not surprised. Culture change takes time, and it's risky. But, we have shifted a number of the rows already, and we will achieve the rest. We've noticed that, as people see the value of the shifts in culture we've already achieved, momentum is making the rest easier. And, we found that many people in our businesses already knew of the problems our strategy is solving. They're glad we've found a better way of doing things.

And, that better way of doing things comes with a cultural shift that is on the one hand subtle, but on the other makes all the difference. From an investment perspective, the energy in our old culture was centered on the beginning of the process - on making the business case for change, and getting it approved. Now, our energy is centered on the end of the process - on everyone exploiting the investments we finish, as much as they possibly can. It is now harder to get a project approved, and more probable it will be cancelled along the way. On the other hand, people know that the changes that we give them to exploit will be the ones most likely to succeed, and we reward them for finding innovative ways of creating value from the changes we invest in.

Some of our local executives struggled with the changes in culture, and behaviors, that we expected them to lead by example. I think they liked the old way better. They have all chosen to leave the company, sometime in the last two years, and, with our customary 'do a good one', we wished them well.

Those executives have not been the only people trying to convince us the old way was better. On reflection I ought to have treated with more care the question I was asked at our conference, about how many other companies are doing it the way we do now. The reason I answered that I didn't care was because I don't believe the number of people doing something a particular way means that's the best way to do it. I prefer to observe, and learn from, the people at the very top their game, which may be many or few. Our people know we are reaching that status ourselves, while other enterprises are still struggling. But, they get challenged by outsiders trying to tell them we are doing it wrong, and that we should - in effect - change back. It puts a strain on their motivations to keep going, and to finish the changes we've started. I, too, get told we're doing it wrong. But, my resolve is unshakeable. We are winning in our strategy. We have diagnosed and are changing our Investment Culture, we have escaped the Project Probability Paradox, and we are delivering the value and structure we need, more risk-efficiently every day. We have unleashed our enterprise to create value from change. That's what gets me up in the morning, and sends me to sleep at night.

The scenario Wendy described in Australia is now a reality. I'm increasingly asked to speak at CEO conferences, about Enterprise Investment and creating value from change. There are still some sharp intakes of breath when I tell people what we have done, and what we have stopped doing. But, I see some people nodding and smiling, and a few come up to me afterwards and tell me they wish they could do the same. I always ask them, rhetorically, "So, what's stopping you?"

I can report that Simon, Lucy, Ivan and Becky are all doing great in their roles. With the rest of us, they are growing and learning all the time. We see them here in New York from time-to-time. Mostly, they are travelling the world, working with their colleagues in our Capability Networks. Lucy and Ivan have created our Sourcing network. At the moment, we have kept HR separate from it, while we conclude whether they actually do sourcing or something else. So, Sam is still my SVP of Human Resources, and still the only one who knows me as Mikey.

Simon, Becky and Ivan transformed the old Enterprise Architecture network into Enterprise Investment. We've had a recruitment program for Investment Project Managers, both within the company and externally. They are still hard to come by, so often we take on Implementation Project Managers and retrain them. For our Enterprise Architecture projects, we assign an Enterprise Architect to manage the outcome and investment, rather than an Investment Project Manager.

Out there, Ivan and Becky have also acquired the nicknames Batman and Catwoman. Both of them are OK with that - it's a cultural thing in itself, and they know it could be much worse!

We did do Lucy's IT transformation project. But, we achieved the outcome we needed for $19 million, not $87 million, by redesigning the change and better leveraging our existing investments. Now, both our customers and our employees are exploiting the results in ways that Lucy and Howard could never have calculated.

All in all, it's amazing what can happen when you have an idea in the bathtub, the shower, the car, the garage or wherever. Enterprise and investment is what turns those ideas into value, or throws them in the trash. My enterprise, yours, everyone's. Nurture it, give it goals, give it space, give it structure. And, of course, protect it from doing us harm.

It feels like we've entered a new era. Capital used to be at the center of our investment culture. Now we treat it, correctly, as one factor in the production of value. Our culture's new center is Enterprise.

Enterprise Investment. Enterprise Architecture plus Investing in Change. Delivering, efficiently, our goals for both value and structure. Coupled with a Sourcing strategy for today's 'cloud' organizations. The CIO and CTO transformed into senior, Board-level roles. Chief Officer for Enterprise Investment. Chief Officer for Sourcing. IT deeply integral to their roles, my role, everyone's role.

Just as it should be.

-END-

Observations

- Treat every cent as an investment, whether it's in today's operations, or in changes for tomorrow and beyond

- Make sure all your portfolios are built using same data model, so that you can aggregate your investment data

- A portfolio is alive, changing all the time (not a static account of your projects)

- Look out for 'Blue Pill Projects' that need to move between value types

- Plan for your projects to overshoot your goals

- Use gross value and costs, not net value, to choose and monitor investments - even for investments with a financial return

- Expect to focus your investments more on leading indicators of value than trailing ones

- Make sure your culture is centered on the end of the investment process, not the beginning.

APPENDIX

Investment Culture Diagnosis

What it All Means

Dimension		Prevailing Culture
Value Creation	Considered Always	Projects consider the creation of value throughout the investment process
	Considered Last	Projects consider the creation of value at the end of the investment process
	Avoided	Projects avoid considering the creation of value
	Considered First	Projects consider the creation of value at the beginning of the investment process
Innovation Focus	None	The company has no explicit focus on innovation
	Market	The company focuses on innovating in the market
	Technical	The company focuses on innovating technically
	Internal	The company focuses on innovating internally
Investment Portfolio	Inventory	The 'portfolio' is an inventory of projects, not grouped by investment goals
	Bottom-Up	Projects are conceived of, grouped by goal, then selected for investment
	Non-Existent	There is no portfolio, or inventory of projects
	Top-Down	A portfolio of investment goals drives the conception and selection of projects
Targeting	Outcomes	Projects are targeted by their value contribution
	Activities	Projects are targeted by their completion of agreed activities
	Outputs	Projects are targeted by their delivery of outputs (e.g. business change, technology)
	None	There is no pattern in the targeting of projects
Exploiting Assets & Services	Central	The enterprising exploitation of assets & services is central to roles and rewards
	Missing	The enterprising exploitation of assets & services is missing from the culture
	Peripheral	The enterprising exploitation of assets & services is peripheral to roles and rewards
	Intended	The enterprising exploitation of assets & services is intended but not realized
Investment Strategy	Random	Each investment is selected on its individual merits
	Strategic Goals	The company's strategic goals drive the selection of investments
	Operational Goals	The company's operational goals drive the selection of investments
	Something Else	Something other than strategic/operational goals drives the selection of investments
Sponsorship	Accountable	Sponsors are materially rewarded or sanctioned if their projects succeed or fail
	Nominal	Projects have named sponsors, who play little or no role in driving success
	Absent	Projects do not have sponsors
	Responsible	Sponsors drive the success of projects, but are not accountable for the outcomes
Project Management	Delivering Change	Project managers are measured on the successful implementation of change
	Time/Cost/Quality	Project managers are measured on time, cost and quality
	ROI Hypothesis	Project managers are measured based on the proposed Return on Investment
	Delivering Value	Project managers are measured on the value their projects deliver
Impact on Operating Costs	Important	A project's costs to P&L materially influences the investment decision
	Ignored	A project's costs to P&L does not feature in the investment decision
	Interesting	A project's costs to P&L feature in the investment decision but have no influence
	Critical	A project's costs to P&L are a determining factor in the investment decision
Behavior Towards Projects	Controlling	People seek to control projects in which they are not a direct stakeholder
	Influencing	People seek to influence projects in which they are not a direct stakeholder
	Undermining	People seek to undermine projects in which they are not a direct stakeholder
	Not Interested	People are uninterested in projects unless they are a direct stakeholder

2483464R00113

· Printed in Great Britain
by Amazon.co.uk, Ltd.,
Marston Gate.